MANCHESTER

The Golden Years

First published in Great Britain by True North Books Limited

England HX3 6SN

01422 244555

www.truenorthbooks.com

Printed and Bound by Short Run Press Ltd, Exeter.

The publishers would like to thank the following companies for their support in the production of this book

---

MAIN SPONSOR

THE PFA

"A brief history of the Professional Footballers' Association"

Elcometer

"Providing inspection equipment solutions across the globe"

Go Goodwins

"Travelling the roads in style"

Greater Manchester Funeral Service Ltd

"Caring for families through their difficult times"

Hadfield Wood Recyclers

"The heart of a Manchester family business"

J. Allcock & Sons

"Recycling rubber around the world"

LANXESS

"At the heart of the chemical industry"

M&I Materials Ltd

"Commercialising Materials for Demanding Applications"

Temperature Control

"Reducing energy without compromising comfort"

The Morson Group

"Global recruitment specialists"

Waters Corporation

"Celebrating the past with an eye on the future"

William Hulme's Grammar School

"The best in everyone"

INTRODUCTION

I am proud of my city of Manchester, its people and the pioneers who helped make it what it is today. A city of culture, commerce, science, education, arts, theatre and my field of sport and football and the players union!

Two of the most renowned and successful clubs in the world befitting the birthplace of the Football League and the Players Union here in Manchester in 1888 and 1907. A political hotbed for protest with Peterloo, the Suffragettes, the Labour Party and the birthplace of the TUC 150 years ago!

What better for our crest than the worker Bee! Labour Omnia Vincit - work conquers all! Agitate Educate Achieve! Proud of our past, our resilience our heroes, enjoying our present, our inclusion, our diversity and planning for our future as a "City United".

Enjoy this book and its portrayal of this city's journey and its influence for so much good in our world today!

Gordon Taylor OBE
Chief Executive, Professional Footballers' Association and Honorary President, FIFPro

CONTENTS

VICTORIAN AND EDWARDIAN DAYS

At the start of the 18th century, Manchester was a small, market town with a population of fewer than 10,000. By the end of the century, it had grown almost tenfold. In the 19th century, the population continued to grow unabated, doubling between 1801 and the 1820s and then doubling again between then and 1851, to 400,000 people. This was phenomenal growth transforming Manchester into Britain's second city. Manchester continued to grow steadily down to the end of the century. In 1901 its population stood at around 700,000; only London and Glasgow were greater in size.

This is such a typical scene of a major city at the turn of the last century. The fashion gives away both the age of the photo and the diversity of the people wandering through the Old Shambles in Manchester. The Victoria Hotel can be seen in the background. Here the young woman on the right wears a typical boater-like hat which was worn together with the simple everyday dress consisting of a white blouse and skirt, usually of darker material. The two gents in the centre with top hats and long coats are possibly discussing the politics of the day. The building to the left is Samuel Kenyon's Wine and Spirit Merchants, which was better known as the Wellington Inn. An inn has existed since 1552 when Edward VI was on the throne. At that time it was situated in the Market Place and Shambles. It is now thought to be the oldest building in Manchester. Unbelievably, it has been picked and literally moved twice and is still standing today. When much of the area was extensively damaged during the WWII blitz, the Shambles survived, however bomb damage and the redevelopment of Manchester necessitated the move to where the Wellington is today.

Below and right: The Art Gallery is shown from two angles here and although there are horses and carts in one and trams in the other, the photos are not too far apart in time, as we can see by the tram tracks. The Gallery built in 1823 on Mosley Street for the Royal Manchester Institution, a society for scholars, later transferred to the Manchester Corporation. These two photos will have been taken between 1905 to 1910, with policemen in the centre of the junction ensuring the traffic flows freely and that pedestrians are kept safe. The new Metro-link trams now dominate this thoroughfare and of course the surrounding buildings have changed significantly so it is good to see the substantial presence of the Art Gallery maintain some of the city's consistency over time.

Below: A leisurely stroll could be taken in Birch Fields Park in the early 1900s as it was opened in 1888 by Prince Albert. The land had originally been owned by John Dickenson who then sold it to the company who created Victorian Park. We can see the new parents with their large pram looking towards the photographer and the little chap with his lace collar and jacket scratching his head in wonderment. Over the hedge it looks like the Men's bowling team are competing on the adjacent green.

This first photo is a bustling view of Market Street in Manchester around 1906, with Hope Brothers Store prominent in the background and Samuels the watchmaker just beyond, easily identified by the large external clock above its shop. The tram tracks can be seen inset in the cobbles and the 'criss-cross' of overhead cables above shows a potentially busy route for this form of public transport. But for now, the delivery boys and their carts would bring the goods to the stores and stalls.

View from a different direction of Market Street, we can now see the tram network in full swing, with up to five trams in view. Delivery carts and horse drawn carriages vie for space on the busy thoroughfare whilst pedestrians have to keep their wits about them as they cross. The tram in the foreground is heading for Belle Vue and hopefully picking up passengers en-route. Shops have their sun canopies out to protect their goods from the heat of the day, although most of the public appear to be dressed for colder weather in long coats and hats!

Below: The Cromwell Monument stands proudly in front of the Manchester Exchange Station, seen here around 1910. The station itself was opened in 1884 and was based on the northern boundary with Salford. Trains ran to Liverpool, Newcastle and London as well as other northern towns. The station was closed in May 1969 with services being directed to Manchester Victoria. The monument of Oliver Cromwell stood in this position at the junction of Deansgate and Victoria Street from 1875 until it was transferred to Wythenshaw Park in 1968. This scene today has changed significantly, but if you stood in the centre of the junction and looked towards the bridge you might just be able imagine this old scene around you.

Right: While it stood Poet's corner was probably the most ancient bit of old fashioned Manchester at the end of the nineteenth century. Standing opposite the Grammar school, it was threatening then to tumble over onto the wooden paved street from its timber support. Probably the oldest building in the dilapidated street was the one in this photograph, which used to be the Sun Inn and Poet's Corner. The old tavern as far back as history can be traced. In the 19th century it became the meeting place for a group of poets who came to be known as "The Sun Inn Group". They went on to launch the Lancashire Author's Association. Subsequently the ancient hostelry was divided into two homely shops, as we can see in this photograph. On the right, R Dearman is the local antique dealer. Long Millgate was the principle thoroughfare to reach the Collegiate Church from the North side of the town. It curves towards Todd Street close to the gatehouse that marks the entrance to Chetham's School.

St Ann's Square is named after the church of St Anne, consecrated in 1712 and made of locally quarried red Collyhurst sandstone. This scene has the photographer with his back to the church, looking towards the Richard Cobden bronze statue. Of course we would not see carriages here today in what is now a pedestrian precinct, but in the month of December we would see a Christmas Market running along the length of the view we see here. The building immediately to the right is now Barclays Bank, with Moss Bros a little further along. To the left is the '3' Mobile Phone shop and next door, would you guess, a 'McDonalds'. Central trees on the precinct now obscure the views towards the larger buildings, which seems a shame from such a prestigious vantage point.

Easily recognisable today, Owens College now the University of Manchester, was founded in 1851, named after a textile merchant, John Owens who had bequeathed almost £100,000 (approx £13m today) to build the college. In 1880 it joined the Victoria University and gained an independent charter in 1900s becoming the Victoria University of Manchester. In October 1873 under the presidency of the Duke of Devonshire, the then principal, Professor Greenwood gave a stirring speech in which he included, ..'to that general culture and discipline of intellect which a man owes not so much to himself, as to the society in which he moves'. In the photo we see here there are three young girls to the left in white smock dresses who may have one day attended the college themselves.

As we can see from the photographs on these two pages, Oxford Street was very much the place for entertainment, with The Palace Theatre, The Hippodrome and The new Pavillion all providing high quality theatre and shows. The Palace was know as 'The Grand Old Lady' and opened in 1891 with the ballet, Cleopatra. It attracted many of the celebrities of the time including Laurel and Hardy, Charles Laughton and later Gracie Fields. The Hippodrome was built some years later in 1904. Providing more of a 'variety' concept of entertainment, the acts included the Max Franklin Troupe, The Merions, Zertho's Dogs and a world famous magician, Chung Lin Soo. The building later became the Gaumont Theatre. The New Pavillion Theatre we can see in the photo was originally the St James's Theatre which opened in 1881. The hall was intended for use as a concert hall, and for public meetings, political demonstrations and 'gatherings of other descriptions'. The hall became the New Pavillion in 1908 showing 'talking pictures' but later closed in 1909 and was then demolished.

PICCADILLY

PALACE
PALACE THEATRE
YUKIO TANI
PALACE THEATRE

Above: The shoppers were out in force in Oldham Street Manchester around 1908. Ladies in their long dresses crossed the street, one with her little girl similarly attired. Gents in boaters and flat caps went about their business whilst the chap to the right cleaned up after the horse and cart, a regular sight on the streets of Manchester in these earlier times. The extensive façade of 'J Jones's Showrooms' would welcome all to its sales. Whilst Burnams further along could expect a busy day ahead. This area is still a vibrant retail outlet of the city and the building just beyond the tram to the left is a large clothing outlet. Today the photographer would be standing outside 'The Crafty Pig, Bar and Kitchen', what a surprise he would have!

Below: A cart fully laden with sacks makes its way along Cross Street, as the tram behind heads off to Middleton Road. The chap by the gas lamp sell his copies of the Evening Chronicle with the headlines of 'Buckingham Palace Intruder', which must have drawn a few more readers. It was a typical scene on Cross St with hoards of shoppers looking through the elaborate windows at new fashions and products. It was a sunny day in Manchester and the two gentlemen in the 'boaters' were chatting as the world passed them by. What a busy city scene in Manchester and so long ago.

THE WAR YEARS

Many people in Manchester had long been prepared for a German offensive, but by 1940 as Britain still remained safe many Mancunians began to feel that perhaps it wouldn't happen.

After neighbouring Liverpool was hit on 21 & 22 December, 1940, it was inevitable that Manchester would not escape. Soon after, the German Luftwaffe began their onslaught on Manchester in one of the fiercest raids of the Blitz. Many of the city's fine Victorian buildings were hit in a 48-hour offensive, including the Free Trade Hall - considered a symbol of the city's greatness, the Royal Exchange, Manchester Cathedral, Piccadilly Gardens and Corporation Street.

A scene of devastation was left after the heavy bombing of central Manchester on 23/24 December, 1940. The bombing, locally referred to as the 'Christmas Blitz' totally destroyed several warehouses on Parker Street, including Staines Inlaid Linoleum; Peel Watson & Co and J Templeton & Co. The damage was extensive and the ensuing blazes spread around into Portland Street, helped by strong winds at the time. Fire-fighters from Manchester worked tirelessly to contain the blaze and were helped by a further 3,400 other fire fighters from surrounding areas. Eventually, other buildings had to be 'dynamited' to create fire brakes which finally contained the fire.

The aftermath of the 'Christmas Blitz' was clearly seen on Cannon Street in the days after, the damage and destruction was immense. The first bomb to fall, hit Salford on 29 July, 1940, but nothing could have prepared the people of Manchester for what started, as the dropping of incendiary devices around 1.40pm, which lit up the city centre and enabled the Luftwaffe to better target the city for another five hours. The night after followed the same pattern as overall 288 bombs hit the city, in total.

It was a devastating time for all Mancunians, who lost the heart of the city and the Piccadilly area in just a few hours, in what would have been the Christmas festive season.

M.C.C.D
Salvage
Appeal
Deposit for
Old
Keys,
Trinkets
Etc,

Left: Given the German U-Boat blockades of the British Isles during the war, salvaging any form of item, from paper, bottles, textiles and even 'pig swill' for the war effort was crucial. Here we see a young lady posting a collection of small items, possibly old keys and necklaces, into the Appeal Box provided. She is typically dressed for the time with seamed nylon stockings, below the knee length skirt and 'bobbed' hair. Everything was indispensible, particularly aluminium which could be sourced from old kettles and saucepans. The slogan used for these items was; 'Send your Pans Flying', 5000 make a fighter, 25,000 make a bomber!

Above: Another aspect of the war brought in support from the Americans as can be clearly seen from the side of the truck in this photo, 'Food Flying Squad, USA to Britain'. It was 1941 and this service had been set up by Lady Reading, founder of the Women's Voluntary Service, whose members helped to staff these canteens which fed the firemen, police and rescue personnel after an area had been bombed. The locals also took advantage of the service whilst sadly contemplating the loss of their homes and neighbourhood.

The Womens Auxilliary Air Force was created in 1939 and at its peak had reached over 180,000 members in 1943. Although they did not participate in active combat, they were exposed to the same dangers as any on the 'home front' working at military installations. 'Warship Week' in Manchester took place in February 1942. It was intended to encourage communities to adopt a Royal Navy vessel. Here we see three WAAF's dressed in their uniforms, preparing to launch a promotional scale model of a barrage balloon, possibly to promote local stores and raise funds for the war effort.

It was unlikely that you would see a line of military tanks on the cobbles in fornt of the Northern Assurance Building in Manchester, even during the war years, but this was a special week for Mancunians. It was Albert Square and the 'Tanks for Attack' campign in 1941, another fundraising initiative by the government, to raise much needed money for the war effort. Other wartime campaigns to raise money and awareness included; 'War Weapons Week'; 'Wings for Victory' and 'Salute the Soldier'. The aim was to persuade the people to invest in War Bonds or simply donate what they could afford. As an example of the staggering generosity of Manchester people, during Warship Week in 1942, the sum of £12,500,000 was raised, almost £3 per person on average.

Left: It was 15 August, 1945 and there was general euphoria across Britain as the Second World War was at an end with the unconditional surrender of the Axis powers on 8 May, 1945. But although the fighting was officially over, it did not mean that supply chains had been re-instated or that food and goods were back in the shops. Here we see a long queue for bread of mostly mums and little ones with smiling faces. Rationing was now well understood with restrictions such as four ounces of bacon, two ounces of tea and half an egg per week. As the worlds countries tried to get back on their feet, demand for certain foods increased. In fact bread was rationed by the Labour government for the first time in 1946 and remained in force for two years. Clearly this was affecting deliveries, as there doesn't seem to be enough loaves in the back of this bread wagon to satisfy even half of the queue.

Below: What a crowd had gathered in Albert Square, Manchester on VE Day, 8 May, 1945 and people flooded out onto the streets to rejoice. It was the end of six years of rationing, bombs and the loss of close family members. The official announcement was made by the Lord Mayor from the Town Hall, which was followed by a transmission of King George VI's broadcast. Men stood on the top of Air-raid Shelters rather than crouching in them with their families. The large banner at the back of the crowds paid tribute to the allied armies and the losses they had also suffered.

Left: The Manchester Corporation was an innovative outfit and never one to be put-off by set-backs or obstacles. During WWII, shortages were a major issue for factories and transport companies, with the Corporation experimenting with the use of gas as a means of propelling their vehicles. This example, from January 1940, shows the gas bag on the roof of the bus with the engine adapted to take the gas flow. The gas was usually generated as the bus went along and stored in the bag. This did however result in a significant loss of power. Sometimes when going up a steep hill, passengers had to actually get out and walk. There were of course also limitations of distance and difficulties re-fuelling on route, not to mention the safety issues if naked flames came into contact with the large bulbous canvas bag.

Above and right: The smiling faces of these young school girls in 1939, conceal the reality of life above ground in these terrible days of war. The air raid shelter was attached to their school at Sharston Senior School, as many shelters were. The governments fear of countless fatalities at the commencement of war, prompted them to build shelters at factories, schools and colleges. Even the Victoria Street arches were converted into shelters to provide a degree of safety should the Luftwaffe strike. The shelters were sparse and cramped but that great British resolve ensured people stayed chirpy if only for the younger ones caught up in the dreadful war. Despite the smiles, the war years were a time of anxiety for most children. Many children had to grow up quickly and look after themselves and in cases younger siblings.

We can see here the girls clutching their gas masks to protect against any gas attacks, these are just a few of the 38 million issued by the government during the war, given its real expectation of what could be ' chemical warfare'.

Children lived in fear from the constant threat of air raids. They spent some nights living in the shelters just in case of German bombing raids.

Above: Manchester Corporation not only transported passengers in peace time, but took an altruistic and crucial role during the Second World War, transporting the injured from the bomb damaged areas of Manchester. This vehicle has been equipped with its own stretchers to evacuate patients from hospitals or the injured from damaged streets. It was a much needed service which supported the over worked ambulances and could move a greater number of the less severely injured in a much quicker time. During 1940-41 speed was of the essence as during the heavy Christmas bombing, over 600 people were killed and hundreds more injured. The bus, number 144, was a 32 seater, Crossley Mancunian, one of many in the fleet but unique for its adaptations.

Left: The risk of gas attacks was even further heightened by the warning from Liddell Hart, a government adviser that Britain could expect up to 250,000 deaths in the first few weeks of hostilities. After the mass issue of masks by early summer of 1939, adults and children were trained in their use and they were required to carry them at all times whilst outdoors. Kiddies would take them to school in small cardboard carrying boxes where they would practice using them in strange situations. Here they were being escorted into the rear of a vehicle through an enclosed ramp.

Below: Finally and officially the war was at an end and celebrations of VE day in 1945 were in full swing. The streets had been decorated with bunting and on Aked Street in Ardwick, an air raid shelter had been turned into a Union Jack as a backdrop to the celebrations. As the euphoria spread, celebrations and parties began in the streets the length and breadth of the country, non more so than in Greater Manchester.

Left: A street party in the Newton Heath district of Manchester during VE Day celebrations. Neighbours, mainly women and children, were out in force to celebrate the end of World War Two. A public holiday was granted on 8 May, 1945, to mark the formal acceptance by the Allies of World War II of Nazi Germany's unconditional surrender of its armed forces in Europe. Then the party began, some of the suburbs staged some of the jolliest celebrations. People had put a great efforts into decorating their houses, putting up bunting and displaying patriotic flags and banners. Bonfires, street tea-parties and fireworks, activities were partof a great national outburst of relief and thanksgiving at the end of nearly six years of war.

We talk today of the mass movement of people, but during the war it was children who were evacuated en-mass to the relative safety of more rural areas and forcibly billeted, if necessary, with householders there. It started on 1 September, 1939 and these Manchester children were taken, reluctantly by their parents or guardians, to the waiting transport, be it train or bus. The children were loaded with small sacks of clothes and maybe a couple of small toys and labelled like goods, in case they became 'misplaced'.

It was a traumatic time for young and old alike, but the servicemen and women ensured that it ran like clockwork. The children would have no idea of where they were being sent and their mothers only hoped that they would at least find a caring family, as many did. It was the unfortunate ones who ended up being skivvy's for families in poorer areas and who could only just make ends meet as it was. These children would write home pleading to be collected. In the case of these children, over half of them would be returned home after only a few months away, as the threats and understanding of how the war was impacting was better understood. Needless to say both the children and parents would have been delighted with the news of their early homecoming.

WORK, REST & PLAY

This scene is definitely not one we would witness today. These dancers at Belle Vue's open air dance platform are 'tripping the light fantastic' on a sunny but cold day. All wearing coats and hats, these happy folk would be fox trotting and gliding on the wooden floor to the popular tunes of the 1930s such as 'Embraceable You' by George Gershwin or 'Love for Sale' by Cole Porter. The boating lake can be glimpsed just beyond the dancers, but there is no sight of the two pleasure boats, 'Little Britain' and Little Eastern' which used to cruise up and down the lake, giving children the thrill of boating. Sadly the wooden dance floor was destroyed by fire in 1958 although it had been used more as a roller-skating rink after WWII.

Below: What a great view of Piccadilly Gardens from Portland Street in 1936, which sadly today would be obscured by the large 6 storey red brick office block of Transport for Greater Manchester. The main buildings in view however still remain, including the Rylands Building, constructed in the 1920s as a warehouse for the Rylands family of cotton manufacturers. Shoppers in 1936 would have found a Woolworths store on the corner of Piccadilly and Oldham Street, shown on the far right of the photograph. It had been built in 1926, replacing the Albert Hotel.

Below: The lads of Manchester at the turn of the last century, learned what a working life was, very early on. This young chap, in barefeet, was in charge of the horse which pulled Horrocks door to door groceries cart, selling amongst other things, the staples of milk and bread. The horse would have been well cared for, as we can see here, as it was the only means of delivering the groceries to the customer. Don't forget, it was a time of very few cars and public transport was unlikely to reach the outskirts of Manchester for some time. The lad may be the son of the grocer, or one who just needed to earn a few pence to help out at home, rest assured he would have loved that horse.

Now we can see the 'Little Eastern' pleasure boat as mentioned earlier, on the lake, at Belle Vue pleasure park around 1952. The park, lakes and grounds were extremely popular for families, particularly during the school holidays. A main attraction over the years was the zoo which was opened in 1836 and could be seen adjacent to the zoological gardens. Sadly, the zoo fell victim to increasing costs which couldn't be met and had to close in the 1970s. The park was later closed in 1982. This was a reflection of the changing attitudes to local entertainment but a real loss to local communities.

This relaxing scene in Piccadilly Gardens in 1955 shows possibly a few office workers taken a well earned rest at lunchtime, plus a few older shoppers who have taken the opportunity to rest their weary legs in the sunshine. The gardens were a real attraction for Mancunians, with extensive flower beds and well manicured lawns across a large area of Piccadilly. You would need to travel back in time over 100 years to find a scene which could be almost as tranquil. It would be around 1812 when this exact area was a quiet residential area known as Lever's Row, a name derived from the Lever family of Alkrington who owned large plots of land in the area at the time. Of course this area has changed significantly these days with the fountain display being the central point, but a deckchair might still fit close by!

Belle Vue Stadium played host to the All England Schools Athletics Championships in 1955 on a bright and sunny day. There were many young men and women proudly representing their schools as they marched passed the judges podium. The track and field championships have been held every year (apart form the war years) since 1925 and are the 4th largest in the world. In this year many would have been inspired by the great Roger Bannister who only months earlier had broken the four minute mile barrier, running the 'Mile of the Century' in 3min 59.4 secs. More recent sporting successes who attended what is now the English Schools' Athletic Championships would include Mo Farah, Kelly Holmes, Jessica Ennis and Greg Rutherford.

Salford Docks
1970s

In its heyday, the Port of Manchester had grown to become one of the busiest ports in Britain and saw exotic goods brought in on the famous Manchester Liners. The docks, which spanned Salford, Stretford and Manchester, helped the region become an industrial powerhouse. They began life in 1894 following the completion of the 35-mile Manchester Ship Canal, an engineering feat that connected the city to the sea. Up to 5,000 people worked at the docks in their heyday. Only a few years before this photograph was taken in 1951, Manchester Docks were Britain's third busiest port owing to damage suffered by the Port of Hull during the Hull Blitz. Competition for jobs was fierce and the stevedores who unloaded the ships had to work in freezing conditions as they kept the city supplied with goods in mid-winter. During the 1970s however the docks began a rapid decline, largely due to containerisation. The increasing size of freight-carrying ships meant they could no longer navigate the ship canal and this, combined with increased trading with Europe and the east, saw use of the docks decrease.

Bank Holiday in 1949. The original 19th century amusement park at Belle Vue dates back to the 1870s and consisted of a small range of attractions that would have been found at many such pleasure gardens at the time. It was in the 1920s and the 1950s that the amusement park took shape and became a worthy competitor to Blackpool Pleasure Beach with its array of death defying attractions and latest technological marvels, coupled with the seaside atmosphere of the flea circus, fairground games and side shows. From the thrilling 'Bobs' ride, so called because it cost a shilling to ride, to the more relaxed Scenic Railway, there was something for everyone. Just after the war when Belle Vue was at its peak. Easter weekends were especially popular with 250,000 visitors through the gates. Our photo shows the fun fair with the Scooter and Caterpillar rides in the foreground and the ever-popular Bobs roller coaster looming large in the distance.

Firework Island on the lake at Belle Vue was the hub of all celebrations held there every 5th November. For many years either side of the second world war this was the place to be to witness huge displays of pyrotechnics as gigantic Catherine wheels whirled, figures on metal frameworks burst into colourful life as sparks showered the night sky and mammoth rockets thundered into the sky drawing oohs and aahs from the massed multitude below. The fireworks were made in their own firework factory. The island was not limited to firework displays, nor did it just function on one day each year. There were battle enactments as great events in British and world history were recreated, often including lots of bangs and crashes to use up the leftover gunpowder from the previous Bonfire Night. In the mid 1950s the firework displays were toned down and, naturally, the public's taste for something more sophisticated took them towards more dramatic entertainment. Audiences dwindled and the last rip was rapped in 1969.

The policeman on traffic duty in Chorlton-on-Medlock, seems to have caused a bit of a tram-jam, as he allows traffic to turn right into Oxford Road from Cavendish Street. Four trams are queuing at at least another two are on the way. On the corner is the distinctive Grosvenor Picture Palace, a former cinema more recently refurbished as the Footage, a Stonegate pub. Built in 1913–15, it was the largest cinema outside London in its day. Described at the time as "Roman-Corinthian of the later Renaissance influence", it was operated by the H.D. Moorehouse chain. The Star Cinema Group acquired the building in the early 1960s and used it for both cinema and bingo. It was never a commercial success due to its distance from Manchester's city centre and was later used as a snooker club for several years before being boarded up. We can accurately date this photograph to 1937 when the American musical film 'Varsity Show' was released by Warner Bros.

Right: The corner shop has been a British institution for hundreds of years. At one time there was only one kind of shop in Britain, small shops independently run by a family who lived above the premises. As cities and towns expanded quickly people began to live further and further away from the central shopping areas. When rows or terraces of new houses were built, the end of the row was almost always built as a shop. These often had a door on the corner of the building rather than at the front. Before the advent of fridges, freezers and products that could be stored for months on end, people would need to be able to easily walk to their local shop to buy what they needed on a daily basis. The shopkeeper would get to know his regular customers as the corner shop often served just a small number of streets. He knew what goods they were likely to buy, and he knew who he could trust to buy groceries on credit during the week with a promise to settle the bill on pay-day.

Below: Aah! that delectable smell of malt extract: all sugar and yeast and... umm, fish livers. A queue young boys, wait their turn to sample a tablespoonful of sweet, treacly gloop, it takes us back to our childhood. Swallowing the magic elixir was supposed to ward off colds and winter illness while building up our weakling bodies. The gloop was a product of the brewing industry, derived from barley grains. Malt extract is packed full of sugars and some nutrients, including vitamin A and riboflavin. After the war it was popular as a cheap dietary supplement for a generation of undernourished children who needed a high carbohydrate feed as well as more vitamins. Back then, its rich, sweet flavour was often combined with unpalatable but nutritious cod liver oil which, with high vitamin D levels, could protect against rickets. An ordeal, but the quicker they took their medicine, the quicker they could get back to playing out with their mates.

Many of us will have seen the iconic American photo of workmen sitting on a girder having lunch, some 840 feet from the ground, as they built the Rockefeller Centre in New York in 1932. Well we in Manchester can boast similar bravery as we see in this comparable photo from 1962. The men are over 380feet from the ground as they enjoy their tea break and whilst reading newspapers. They are involved in the construction of the CIS Tower on Miller Street in Manchester, which at the time of completion was the tallest in the city and the second tallest office building outside London. The tower was designed as a prestige headquarters to showcase the Co-operative movement in Manchester. Today, only one building in Manchester is taller and that is the Beetham (Hilton) Tower, Deansgate, completed in 2006 which is also the tallest building outside London. Two other proposed buildings for Manchester would have even surpassed these, the River Street Tower and the Piccadilly Tower, but neither have yet been built.

Maine Road, one of the most famous grounds in the country, stands like an oasis amidst the surrounding housing in this aerial view of 1970. In its earlier incarnations, under the names of St Mark's (West Gorton), Gorton AFC and Ardwick FC, Manchester City had a number of homes including Clemington Park, Reddish Lane and Hyde Road. Whilst at the latter ground the club adopted its present name, and paid £5,500 for the site of an old brickworks at Moss Lane. The new stadium of Maine Road arose from the rubble in 1923, a venue not only good enough for an ambitious club, but grand enough also for FA Cup Semi-Finals. Safety standards were not as strict in those days, and the ground saw some colossal attendances. When Stoke City visited the ground to play Manchester City in a cup game in 1934, the gate was a huge 84,569. Because of its high capacity, it gained the nickname 'Wembley of the North'. Maine Road as pictured in 1970 was a ground that was graced by the exciting attacking skills of Lee, Bell and Summerbee. City had won the League Championship in 1968 and the FA Cup in 1969. In 1970 the club lifted the European Cup Winners Cup.

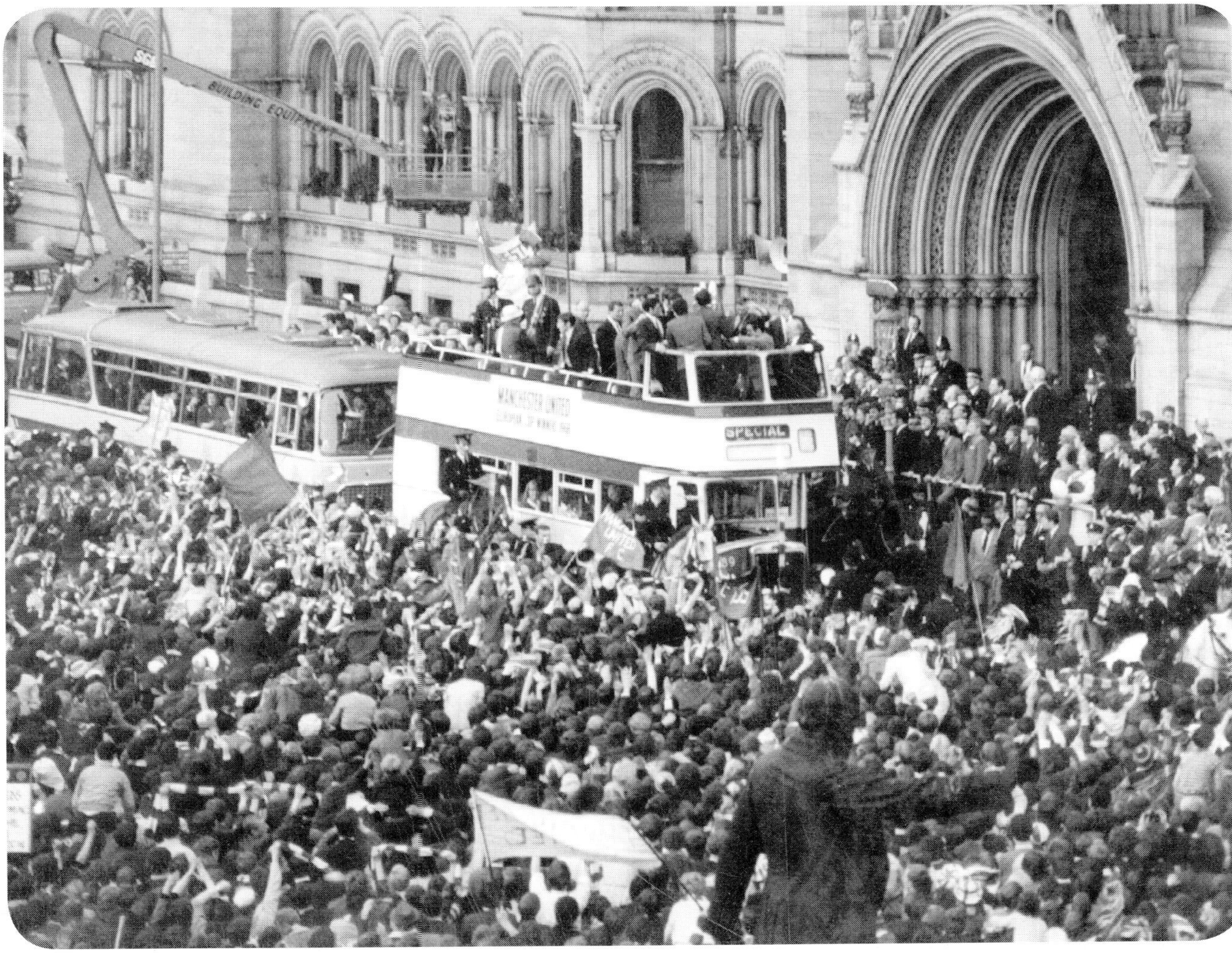

Some would say this was the height of Sir Matt Busby's reign at Manchester United, bringing home the much coveted European Cup. After losing in semi-finals previously, this win was made all the sweeter as this much vaunted team beat the mighty Benfica 4-1 after extra-time at Wembley on 29 May, 1968. A goal in normal time by Bobby Charlton was soon matched by Benfica. In extra-time, George Best scored, followed by the 19 year old birthday boy, Brian Kidd and then Charlton again to confirm the great win. The game had been followed by thousands of fans and Mancunians alike. The crowds we see here outside the Town Hall cheered the team incessantly as they arrived for the civic reception, led by mounted police.

HEINZ
TOMATO

This was a typical scene on match day at a major football ground at the end of the 1950s. It was Warwick Road in Manchester at the end of the season in 1959 after the game most likely to have been against Birmingham City which United won 1-0. The club and supporters were still grieving over the tragic loss of eight players in the Munich air disaster of February 1958. Sir Matt Busby, as he later became known had brought the struggling team of the early 1950s to glory in recent years with League Championships in 1952, 1956 and 1957. This season saw the team finish 2nd in the league with Bobby Charlton playing in 38 games and scoring 29 goals. As many as a dozen buses wait in line for fans to come rushing out of the ground at the full time whistle, heading for the city centre and probably a pint or two.

Below: George Best, Manchester United's young mop-topped winger, doesn't just confine his genius to the football field, as can be seen here in this photograph with rival and close friend Mike Summerbee of Manchester City. Together they opened a number of fashion boutiques in Manchester which were run by Malcolm Mooney. He ended up having a stake in all three shops, as well as 'Edwardia' in Sale, he also had a shop just off Deansgate and a third in the Arndale Shopping Precinct. Best also ventured into the travel agency business and opened a couple of nightclubs, Slack Alice's and Oscars.

Left: This photo is as interesting as much for the fans clamouring for autographs beneath the sign reading three shillings (15p) to watch the first team, which seems extremely cheap compared to todays prices. It was Manchester City's ground in 1950 when these young fans had spotted Bert Trautmann, the Manchester City goalkeeper. He was in fact born in Germany and had joined the Luftwaffe as a paratrooper earning medals including the iron cross and was captured by the British towards the end of the war. He refused repatriation to Germany and settled in Lancashire and became a well respected sportsman. He was named Footballer of the Year in 1956 and had played and won the FA Cup that year, having played for nearly 20 minutes after a collision with a Birmingham City player, with what later was found to be a broken neck. Trautmann made 545 appearances for Manchester City through his career with them. He was awarded an OBE for his promotion of Anglo-German understanding through football and died at the age of 89 in July 2013.

Above: This was the local derby game of 1967 when the two Manchester rivals met at City's ground in 1967. We can see the athletic Bobby Charlton as he fires the ball passed the Mulhearn, who had recently arrived from Stockport and had admitted he was nervous, for the first of his two goals. City had scored first through their key player Colin Bell, after five minutes and it was credit to Manchester United that they came back to lead 2-1 at half time. The match was watched by over 60,000 fans with no further goals in the second half. Advertising banners always brought in much needed money and given the crowds sizes clearly Picks (for Ford), Granville's and Old Charlie Rum, felt it was worth putting their names on the roof of the stands.

THE PFA

A brief history of the Professional Footballers' Association

When the Football League was formed in 1888, issues such as the retain and transfer system which prevented a player leaving a club freely even after his contract had ended, the £4 maximum wage and the lack of compensation for injuries, meant players' felt they were not being represented fairly and professional football was not even recognised as a profession under the Workmen's Compensation Act.

However, after early attempts to organise the players had been unsuccessful, the then footballing light Billy Meredith of Manchester United and Welsh international, a born leader, chaired the inaugural meeting of the footballers' trade union at the Imperial Hotel in Manchester on December 1907 and became the figure head the players needed at that time.

The new union saw its aim as not just financial and contractual freedom, but also the creation of a body that would help all professional footballers, no matter what their station, to obtain justice in disputes with their clubs, a restitution in the case of injury and punishment.

However, it wasn't long before it found itself in direct conflict with its parent body the Football Association (FA) with its decision to affiliate to the National Federation of Trade Unions.

Fearing the players would one day resort to strike action, the FA withdrew its support from the union and demanded that every player resigned from it or be exiled from the game. Manchester United and other players led by captain Charlie Roberts, refused to comply and were suspended by their clubs.

The players and their stance became a battle of wills, which culminated in a stand-off at the beginning of the 1909 - 1910 season. With the League clubs facing the prospects of no games, the FA backed down and the now known "Outcasts" won a famous victory.

The first World War years proved trying with players being called up en masse to the front line often showing great bravery one of whom, Donald Bell, won the Victoria cross; while in World War II whole teams were enlisted to fight.

Cliff Lloyd and George Eastham.

Top: *The Players Union badge.* **Above:** *Jimmy Guthrie leaves Wolves.*

Above: *The "Outcasts".* ***Right:*** *PFA Banner.* ***Below:*** *Player Donald Bell, who won the Victoria cross.*

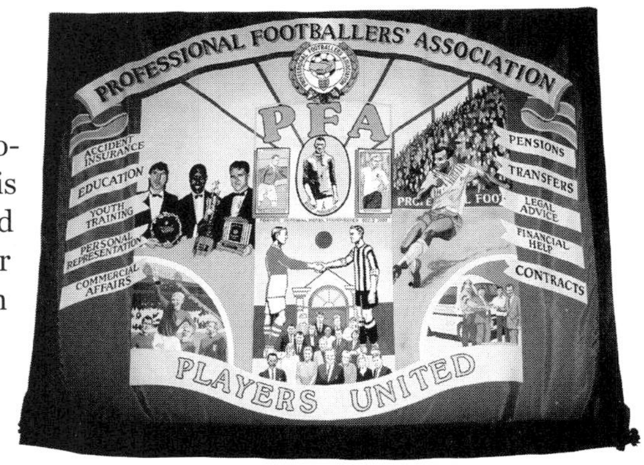

The union's future was threatened as football took a back seat, but the Union survived and after World War II, its role expanded following a massive surge of interest in the game.

The players had failed to reap the benefits of the post-war boom and conditions and football was still a hugely restricted profession without proper welfare, freedom of contract or even acceptable pay. Jimmy Guthrie chairman from 1947, famously referred to players as "modern day slaves" during a highly emotive speech at the 1955 TUC conference in Blackpool.

It would be another 8 years before the main focus of Guthrie's rage, the retain and transfer system was broken but in the meantime the union continued to achieve significant reform within the game.

Secretary Cliff Lloyd, along with Jimmy Hill the Chairman, fought hard for the removal of the maximum wage which was finally abolished in 1961. The maximum a player could earn had gone from £4, set in 1900, to just £20 in almost 60 years. The critics insisted its removal threatened the future of the game, but the removal of the maximum wage is often seen as a pivotal moment in the history of professional football in this country, and five years later England won the World Cup!

The lifting of the maximum wage was but one of a raft of demands put before the Football League by the newly dubbed Professional Footballers Association (PFA). The PFA called for the abolition or at least radical reform of the detested 'retain and transfer contract system'. What the players desperately wanted was the freedom to negotiate their own contracts and the chance to freely walk away when mutually acceptable terms could not be agreed.

Backed by a 100% strike ballot result and knowing he had the media as well as the general public on his side, Hill threatened to bring the game to a complete standstill for the first time in its history.

Above: *The Busby Babes.*

Another important landmark was finally reached in 1963 when the 'retain and transfer system' was finally challenged. Skilful inside forward George Eastham was refused a transfer from Newcastle United to Arsenal.

The system at the time meant that Eastham could be kept at the club on less money than he was being offered by Arsenal. Using the courts along with the solidarity of the members, the PFA launched a test case against the system which was declared unlawful by Judge Wilberforce.

It was the beginning of the end for the system that had blighted the lives of thousands of professional footballers since the turn of the 20th Century. It was a massive decision in many ways and was the forerunner of the transfer system of today. For the first time, players could not be held beyond the end of their contract and to this day it stands as one of the PFA's most significant achievements.

The ground-breaking Chester Committee Report (CCR) on the future of the professional game produced in 1968 also had a significant influence on the PFA. The Committee was set up after the FA and the Football League had called on the government to take action due to the deteriorating financial position of the game.

The reports far reaching suggestions had not been welcomed by football's authorities which had wanted money rather than advice. By contrast it boosted the PFA's growing belief that it had an influential role to play in the future of the game.

The CCR concluded that the PFA "has the peculiar problem of watching over the interests of boys at one end and men whose careers finished in their early thirties at the other".

For the PFA, the CCR was seen as an opportunity for it to tackle diversely related problems such as disciplining players by both the ruling bodies, behaviour of its members on and off the field and their public image, financial security of members, and their education before during and after their playing careers.

The seventies proved to be a very influential decade for the PFA with the Industrial Relations Commission on football chaired by Professor Sir John Wood bringing in many innovations, not least the Standard Contract in 1981 and a new Collective Bargaining Agreement via the Professional Football Negotiating Committee. In 1971 Bob Kerry became the PFA first Education Officer in charge of developing services for any member or ex member wishing to take vocational training. It would lead in 1979 to the formation of the Footballers' Further Education and Vocational Training Society (FFE&VTS).

In 1974 the PFA Awards Dinner was inaugurated, a lavish, black-tie event held in one of London finest hotels in Park Lane and transmitted live by ATV. The players picked as their first Players' Player of the Year winner, Leeds United's Norman "bites your legs" Hunter. The Young player of the year was Kevin Beattie of Ipswich Town Football Club.

Above: *The Bradford City Fire.*

The 1980's were great years for the PFA and its members but the opposite for the game itself. On the terraces, the surge of hooliganism had been wreaking havoc for a decade, the tragic deaths of so many fans in the Bradford City fire, also we saw the tragedies of Hillsborough and Hysel, all of which saw the game plunge into a severe depression. There was also the economic recession that saw many smaller clubs facing bankruptcy.

However, for the PFA and its members it was time of significant change and opportunity. In 1981 the new players standard contract was introduced and for the first time since the 1890s players found themselves free to seek and move to a new club once their existing contract had expired. Negotiations had been long and hard ever since the Eastham judgement in 1963. This system would last until the ground-breaking Jean Marc Bosman case in 1995. It was a historic shift in relationships between players and clubs and marked the start of the modern era for professional players.

In 1980 the players cash benefit scheme was being presented to the players via area meetings. The new scheme provided professional players with something that no other industrial worker had- (apart from deep sea divers and circus performers) a lump sum payment on attaining the age of 35, based on the years of service multiplied by the average earnings, multiplied by 3.75% plus a death in service benefit of up to four-time earnings.

Further benefits followed for members during the next few years and in 1985 a joint initiative between the PFA and the Football League to provide a private contributory pension scheme for all full-time professional footballers was started and known as the PFA and Football League players retirement income scheme. In 1986 the footballers' further education and vocational training scheme (FFE/ VTS) was initiated, one of the three welfare schemes the PFA operated for members.

The additional two were the Benevolent Fund that provided grants to current and former members needing financial assistance and the Accident Insurance Fund, which assisted former players experiencing medical difficulties due to previous injury during their playing career.

Also, in 1986 the Football in the Community scheme was formed by FFE&VTS between the PFA and The Football League, and clubs began developing community schemes offering a wide range of sports and social based activities supported by the PFA. This was the beginning of a nationwide Corporate Social Responsibility Programme unique in the world after a pilot programme with six North West Clubs. Players agreed to contribute up to 6 hours a week for this social inclusion programme.

Above: *PFA Chief Executive, Gordon Taylor.* ***Below:*** *Bus advertisement showing the role of the PFA at the time of the dispute with the Premier League in 2001.*

Throughout the 80's led by Gordon Taylor, the PFA had made strenuous efforts to prevent a break away by the bigger more powerful clubs as they strove to maximise their earnings by retaining a bigger share of match receipts and television and sponsorship income. In 1991 the FA proposed the creation of a Premier League of 18 top teams to be run by an independent management committee but ultimately under the control of the FA.

The PFA response to this was a pointed reminder to all concerned that the players could make or break any such scheme.

After being excluded from the initial negotiations, the PFA armed with a mandate from the club delegates at the 1991 AGM and reinforced by the strength of the subsequent strike ballot amongst the division one members, gave the PFA more than 90% support for a variety of courses of action. The PFA ultimately emerged from the construction of the Premier League in a much stronger position.

On contracts and regulations affecting and protecting players everything remained in place while the new Premier League and the Football Association agreed to join the newly constructed Professional Football Negotiating and Consultative Committee (PFNCC), which had authority to cover all issues affecting the professional game, not just those affecting players, but nothing could be done affecting players without the approval of the PFA!

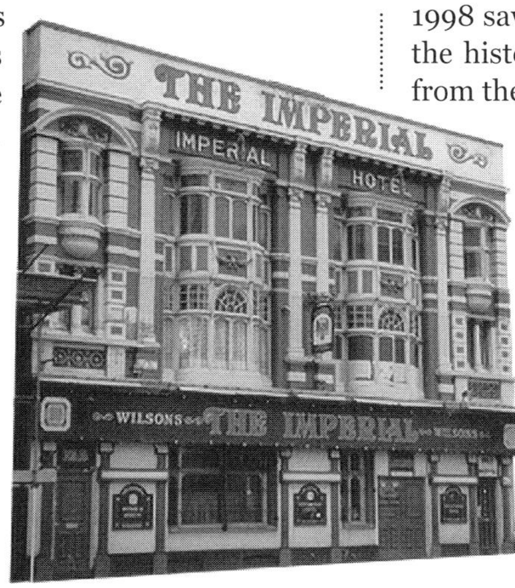

After the construction of the new Premier League in 1992 the PFA's combined television income from the Premier League and the Football League stood at £3Million. Moves by football's governing bodies to reign in this income had already been attempted culminating in 1996 when the Football League tried to reduce its overall payments to the PFA. The association stood resolutely against this and Chief Executive, Gordon Taylor put it to the union AGM in November 1996 by saying "we were met with a very intransigent attitude and clearly the Football League were looking to test our resolve and may well have been supported in this action by the Premier League".

1998 saw the negotiation of the biggest ever television deal in the history of UK sport, the PFA's combined annual income from the TV monies now stood at £9,000,000.

Both the League and the Premier League had negotiated an enormous new deal with BskyB. The Leagues income leapt from £9Million to £25Million a year while the Premier League share rose from £40Million to £180Million per year. The Football League attempted to make the PFA payment a discretionary one but the threat of a strike brought them to the table and agreement was reached on a pay out of just over 5% of the League TV income. With the union strike ballot reaping 91.8% vote support, the FA and the Premier League subsequently matched the League's offer. Things would not be so simple the next time round.

The PFA now became a much bigger player on a much wider scale. In 1995, it accepted an invitation to re-join the TUC. Gordon Taylor had been appointed president of FIFPro the international body of players' union's, an organisation that would begin to play an ever-increasing role in the governance of the game worldwide.

In 2000 the footballing governing bodies negotiated new financial deals with the television companies. The figures were astounding, resulting over a three-year period the Premier League receiving £1.5Billion and the Football League £315Million.

In complete ignorance of the new television deals offered to the FA, The Football League and the Premiership, the PFA were offered a derisory £115,000 on top of their previous deal.

Top: *The Imperial Hotel, Manchester where the inaugural meeting of the footballers' trade union was held.* ***Left:*** *Richard Scudamore of the Premier League with PFA Chief Executive, Gordon Taylor.*

Above: *New set up at FIFPro (World Players' Union 1991).* ***Below:*** *Norman Hunter, 1st PFA Player of the Year 1974.* ***Below right:*** *The Three Degrees of WBA FC, Laurie Cunningham, Brendon Batson and Cyrille Regis.*

Gordon Taylor was threatening industrial action and he later wrote "we believe the football bodies had a political agenda to diminish if not extinguish the status of the PFA and its very existence." In September Gordon Taylor said that he would be consulting his membership and possible strike action, unless the Premiership came up with a serious offer, one that respected previous agreements.

For the next two months there was a remarkable airing of grievances and prejudices within the game culminating in ballot forms being distributed asking for the mandate to strike. In November the ballot produced a vote in favour, which was unprecedented in any industrial action according to Gordon Taylor. Of the 2,496 ballot papers sent out to members 2,290 were returned of which over 99% were in favour of strike action. The vote called for players to boycott matches played in matches in front of TV cameras, either for live broadcast or recorded highlights.

The first high profile game scheduled to be affected was Arsenal v Manchester United on November 25th, but the Premier League asked the PFA for a meeting on the proceeding

Monday. Following a meeting in which it was agreed that the PFA would now receive a basic £17.5 million for 10 years. No strings were attached to the money, thus underpinning the position of the PFA as an independent body beholden to no one.

In 2007 the PFA celebrated its 100th year in existence and the intention was for the world's oldest sporting union to help the world's oldest children's hospital, the University Children's Hospital in Manchester establish a new rehabilitation and physiotherapy unit, together with rooms for parents to stay overnight.

The strap line for the year's events including a pro-celebrity golf day, two race days, a national keepy-uppy competition culminating with a Legends match between England versus World X1 followed by a gala dinner, was ONE GOAL, ONE MILLION. One Million pounds was aimed for and One Million pounds was achieved and paid for a new hospital wing, allowing parents to stay overnight next to their children.

As we enter the second decade of the second century in the PFA history as it begins to unfold, the radical changes in the status, nature and character of its membership have presented challenges and opportunities its founders could never have dreamed of.

A role model for other unions and guardian of the games populist heritage, an agent in its transformation in terms of image and appeal, the PFA is now an

Top: *Football legends, David James, Steven Gerrard and David Beckham at the PFA Centenary Year 2007.* ***Left and below:*** *As part of the ONE GOAL, ONE MILLION, a gala dinner took place and the PFA celebrated its 100th year.*

***Top:** Making the Transition 2018, held at the Leicester Marriott hotel supporting members to prepare for the future.* ***Below:** FL Community Player of the Year Reda Johnson, Sheffield Wednesday sponsored by the PFA.*

integral part of the nation's sporting fabric. It's been a long, hard journey, but one Billy Meredith would have been thrilled to see completed in such style.

Modern footballers are in a hugely privileged position, but they owe a debt of gratitude to their predecessors who have helped put them where they are today.

Today the future looks very bright. We have a voice across the whole of football and proud to be the oldest and strongest sporting union in the world. As we move forward it is important to remember what has come before us, where we are now and where we plan to be in the future protecting our players and protecting our game.

We should never lose sight of the importance of our history. Only by looking at where the game has been in the past can we come to best judgement about where it should go in the future.

We are the most cosmopolitan football country in the world, diverse and inclusive. We research medically, we care for our members past and present, we negotiate for the future. We have the most full time professional football clubs in the world, the most professionals and the highest attendances and TV & Commercial income. We are the world's most popular participant and spectator sport and shall continue to be "worker bees" to keep it that way!

ON THE MOVE IN MANCHESTER

Below: Here we have a photo of the early London Road station as it was called in the early 1900s, although there have been considerable changes to the city centre and much building work has taken place over the last century, the main station continues on. Transport hubs in city centres generally have a great deal of infrastructure supporting them and Piccadilly Station is no exception. Of course the horse and carts we can see have long since gone and the carriages through the centre of the main road to the station have now been replaced with several taxi ranks. It is a wonderful view of a cities transport network and you may be able to sense the grandeur of Manchester in these early industrial days. The building to the left is the Northern Railway Company's Goods Station with the main building directly in front being built in the mid 19th century. Tram lines can be seen along the cobbled London Road, albeit with no trams in sight. Today the station, renamed Manchester Piccadilly in 1960, continues to be a central transport link for Manchester managing a staggering 27 million passengers per year.

Above: There is more to this picture than first meets the eye, it was one of Manchester first taxi's! The service was run by the appropriately named, Quick family and operated from the fountain in Ashton-in-Makerfield. Not known to many and given the size probably seriously underpowered, it was a 15 horse power Fiat Landaulette which seated six passengers very easily. The rag wrapped spare tyres on the side of the vehicle look like late editions but would certainly be needed given the poor road conditions of the time. It was a start for Harry Quick and the company soon grew into a large operation with an extensive number of private hire cars and the buying and selling of new models. Quicks Group PLC was quoted on the stock market in 1947 and grew to one of the country's largest motor groups with over 2,500 employees.

Left: A rather glum looking Neville Staniar of John Staniars Wire company founded in Manchester in 1790, is at the wheel of a grand looking car around 1905. We know the photo has to be later than 1903 as that is when vehicle number plates were introduced and the one we see here is 'N 904' and would be worth thousands of pounds in today's market. His passenger is his daughter Gwennie in what is thought to be an early Sunbeam 4 cylinder vehicle. The little Jack Russell dog in the front seems happy enough.

Below: In this busy 1946 scene the horse and cart looks in a very dangerous situation as they try to manouvre across the traffic, between the Pilcher tram and the No16 Monton bus heading straight towards them. Even after the war, the noble horse was still to be found as part of the transport system in urban areas. In back streets rag and bone men came round in their carts, chimney sweeps came with their tackle and window cleaners arrived bearing their ladders, buckets and 'shammy' leathers. Gardeners eagerly awaited their appearance as they prepared to sweep up behind them, searching out additives for their rhubarb and roses. To the right, a handsome Rolls Royce acts as a fiscal contrast to horse and cart. Victoria Station approach is to the left. Manchester Cathedral dominates this part of Victoria Street. Built in a perpendicular, Gothic style, the cathedral marks the centre of medieval Manchester. It was dedicated by Henry V to St Mary, St Denys and St George.

Left: Chryslers in Manchester were originally sold by William Grimshaw and family, with William having started out firstly in gramophones and then cycles before taking on a dealership for Maxwells Cars, which later became Chryslers. This photo from what is believed to be the Manchester city showrooms before the company moved to Cateaton Street in Manchester in October 1929. The new showroom had artificial lighting and a large show hall for the twenty or so cars which would be displayed there. Grimshaws became a very successful car retailer, with a catch phrase of 'Every model a masterpiece'. At the time a six cylinder model could be bought for £299 and an eight cylinder for £577 (around £35,000 today).

Below: One of the earliest flights to have taken place in Manchester was by the Staniar Glyder, constructed by Staniars Wire company. A major part of their early production was fine wire products and silk mesh. The silk covered the wings of this aeroplane which was built at the Staniar factory and exhibited in Heaton Park around 1910. Its intrepid pilot was seated at the controls, cap on reversed, with his right hand on the release lever and with the large wooden propeller just behind him. It would have been a momentous time for these young aviators and no doubt the onlookers would have wished them well.

Left: Alliott Verdon Roe set up one of Britain's most prestigious aviation manufactures in Manchester in 1910 with his brother Humphrey and the company trade name AVRO, was soon derived from the founders initials.
Ancoats Lane was the companies first premises before it moved through several sights before establishing itself in the Newton Heath factory at the end of the first world war. It seems odd to see a horse and cart transporting an aeroplane, but this is what we have in this photo. It was a Type E aircraft which was being taken to the, then London Road station (now Piccadilly Station) for the train journey to Brooklands in Surrey for test flying.

Above: Arguably the world's first bus service with horse drawn minibuses was started by John Greenwood in Manchester and ran between Market Street and Piccadilly and Pendleton Toll Gate. The turn of the last century saw a real growth in the city of Manchester and consequently the transport infrastructure which was needed to support this. This fine old photograph from 1902, shows two early horse drawn trams and a 'bowler hatted' conductor leaving the tram to switch the tram tracks to another direction. Gents and ladies can be seen on the top deck of the trams which were always popular on dry sunny days as they head out to Old Trafford or Bell Vue. We would certainly feel sorry for the two horses, today, who had a considerable weight to haul, particularly with a full passenger load. It was in the operators interest however to look after their animals and ensure they were well fed and watered and could be changed over on route if necessary.

An early 1930s photo of Deansgate in Manchester, shows the cars of the time mingling with the trams and horse and carts. The building to the right on the corner is the red bricked Elliot House, now home to the Greater Manchester Chamber of Commerce. Immediately opposite is Oddfellows House, this building now provides two restaurants but was previously occupied by the Inland Revenue. New office blocks have taken the place of the buildings on either side of the tram but the castellated building just beyond on the left is the John Rylands Library opened in 1900. It was founded by Enriqueta Rylands in memory of her husband. The library is now part of the University of Manchester Library.

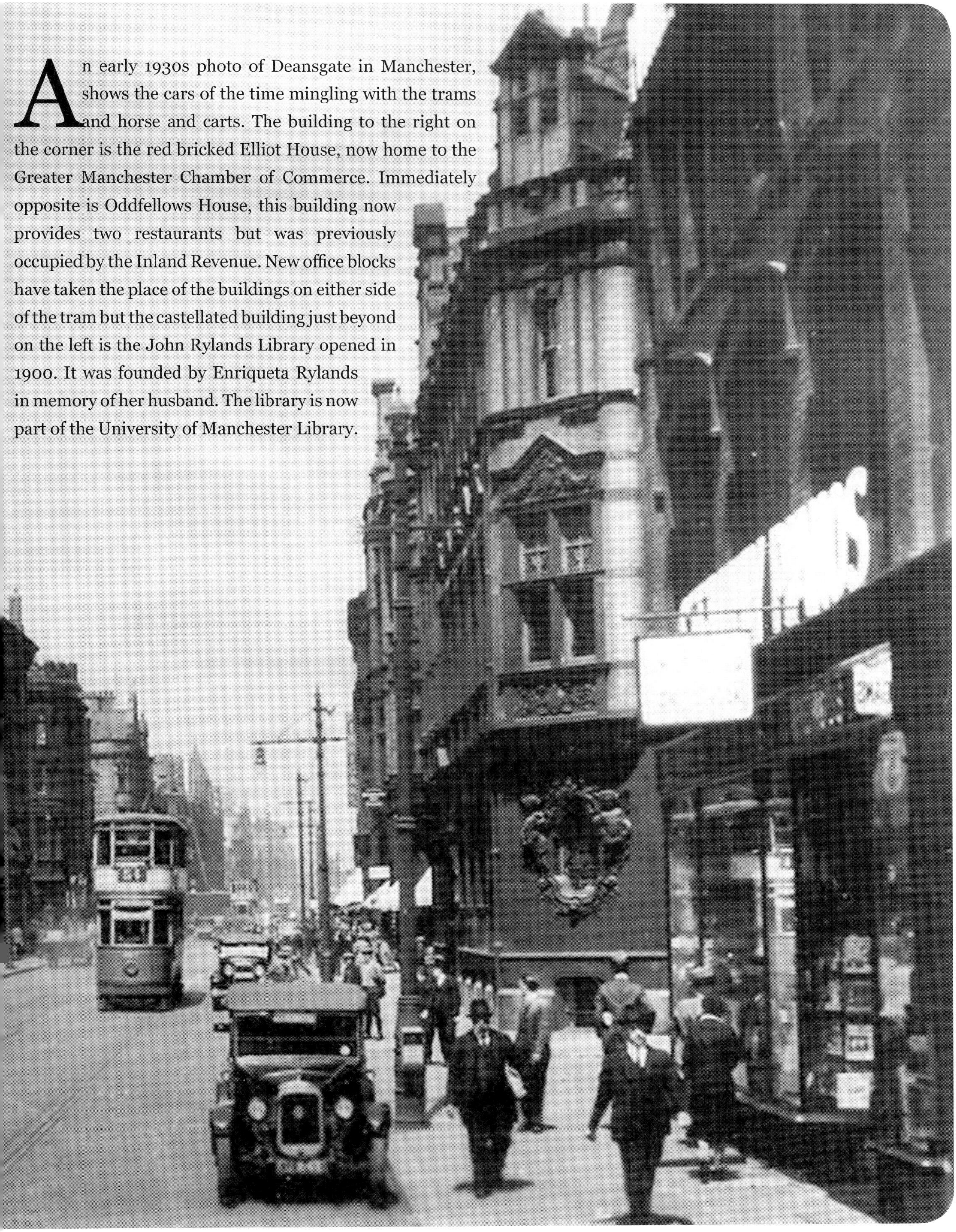

Lewis's store, that was in business from 1877 to 2001 on the corner of Market Street and Piccadilly, was a favourite meeting place for a girl and boy who were 'walking out' together in 1957 if they came from different suburbs in Manchester. The store arcade was just around the corner from the bus stands and many a young man waited patiently for his sweetheart to arrive on a Saturday night. Then it was off to one of the burgeoning coffee bars that had a jukebox where the couple could sit at a table over a couple of frothy cups and gaze into each other's eyes. Tab Hunter's 'Young love' described their feelings for each other quite admirably. Couples would move on to spend the evening dancing at the Ritz Ballroom or on the back row at any of a large number of cinemas in the city. When it came time to say goodbye, they walked back to the bus station, shared a goodnight kiss and arranged to meet next week, same time, same place. This was all witnessed by Sir Robert Peel, from the plinth where his statue had stood since the middle of the previous century.

This is a relatively quiet traffic scene along Oxford Road, probably in the late 1950s. This section of Oxford Road is easily recognisable with the Regal Cinema building on the right. Originally opened as the Twin Regal Kinemas in 1930, the cinemas each had separate entrances and foyers. Shortly after this picture was captured, they were bought by the Star Cinemas group and renamed Romulus and Remus, which lasted just two years before they became known as Studios 1 & 2. Today it is identifiable as, The Dancehouse arts and film venue. Many readers will have had lessons from the BSM Driving School premises on the corner of Oxford Road and Hulme Street and travelled up and down this road hundreds of times no doubt. Driving along this road today, by far the biggest problem is not driving in the designated bus lanes. In one year motorists have been caught out a staggering motorists have been caught out nearly 350,000 times.

These are two interesting views of St Peter's Square, looking from different angles. Free flowing traffic moving around the Square plays a big part in both photographs. The north of the square is bounded by Princess Street and the south by Peter Street. To the west of the square is Manchester Central Library and the Midland Hotel. In the 1930s, the square was redeveloped around the construction of the Central Library and Town Hall Extension (1930–34). The square is home to the Manchester Cenotaph and incorporates the Peace Garden. The area around St Peter's Square, then known as St Peter's Field, was the site of the 1819 Peterloo Massacre. The name derives from St Peter's Church which was built in 1788-94 where the gardens are today and also gave its name to Peter Street. The Temple Moore's memorial cross to the former St Peter's Church, which occupied the site intended for the war memoria, can be clearly seen in both images. The Manchester Cenotaph is the work of Sir Edwin Lutyens and has similarities to the Cenotaph in Whitehall. It was inaugurated in 1924 and the ceremonies of Remembrance Day have been observed here annually since then.

It's a sunny day in 1957 when the new bus terminus begins to take-on passengers. The corporation are still earning a little money from allowing advertisements on their buses, from St Bruno tobacco to Openshaw Ales. The scene is quite different today as the area has been completely remodelled, although many of the buildings in view still exist. Gone is the Halifax Building Society we see to the left and we have no advert for Mothers Pride bread which we can see here directly ahead. One eyesore from this era was the endless parked cars on the open land to the left, which thankfully disappeared in the 1960s.

Manchester has played an important part in the production of Ford cars, with the assembly plant in an old Tram factory in Trafford Park, opening in 1911. By 1913, six thousand cars were produced and the Model T became the country's biggest selling car with 30% of the market. Many readers who were Ford car owners in the past, will remember the enormous Manchester Garages building on Oxford Road, opposite Whitworth Park. Riders of the two-wheeled variety take a look at what was happening to the Morris Minor on the garage forecourt, as they pass by. To the left, a Vespa rider passes a parked Ford Anglia, probably produced in the 1940s. Just ahead is another Ford model, the Zephyr Six from the mid-1950s, this gives the image an older look than it probably is. Pump tops branded with the company name, like these for Shell, became the norm by the mid to late 1960s.

A small group of people and a dog had gathered on the roundabout at Canute Square to see the vintage cars pass through Knutsford. They would have been particularly impressed when these early Rolls Royce cars passed, possibly en-route to the firm's original works in Cooke Street, Hulme, Manchester. Unless you've been to the Museum of Science and Industry, you might not know about the connection the city has with one of the world's most celebrated luxury automotive brands. Henry Royce's Manchester connection goes back even further than the automotive age, as he had an electrical and mechanical factory in the city from the 1880s. In 1904 he manufactured his first car in the city, the two-cylinder Royce 10, but the landmark date of that year was in May, when he met Charles Rolls at Manchester's Midland Hotel. Rolls was a car dealer, and by the end of 1904 had placed an order for everything Royce could produce. For an attractive reminder of what Knutsford looked like in times gone by, you need look no further than the thatched and gabled White Bear Inn on Warrington Road. This 16th century pub was popular with coach travellers waiting for The Aurora going north to Liverpool or south to Newcastle, Birmingham and London.

Life was slowly getting back to normal in the centre of Manchester only two years after the end of WWII. This car Park on Mosley Street was almost full when this photograph was taken in September 1947.To the right is Piccadilly Gardens, which has been for many years the central hub of Manchester's public transport system. The fabulous array of different makes of car are parked on the site of what is now the Piccadilly Exchange. This building, beside Parker Street across from Piccadilly Gardens, was designed by Covell Mathews and Partners and built between 1959 and 1965. Lewis's store in the background, stood proudly on the corner of Piccadilly Gardens as one of the city's first department stores which opened in 1877.

Founded by David Lewis, who opened a flagship store in Liverpool originally only selling boys and men's clothing, the department store grew to a country-wide chain.The Manchester store even included a full scale ballroom on the fifth floor, which was also used for exhibitions.

A more 'down to earth' form of transport was of course the bicycle which had been around since the early 19th Century. These chaps have not just happened upon the same park to gather, they are in fact competitors of the Heaton Park 50 mile race in 1950. The race was promoted by Len Myatt and took place in the park on a one and a half mile circuit, several times a year. It is good to see the cyclist on the left wearing a Manchester Wheelers top, a club which still thrives today and has been instrumental in the growth of Manchester cycling over the years. Manchester is of course home to the National Cycling Centre, one of the worlds finest cycling sports venues. It would be nice to think that this Heaton Park race contributed to Britain's overall success in today's world of cycling.

ROYAL VISITS TO THE CITY

What a magnificent group of royals and dignitaries on the steps of what we believe is the Royal Exchange building in 1921, which had recently been remodelled. King George V and Queen Mary look every bit, the royal couple as they stand proudly for the photographer, accompanied by officials of the legal profession, the Lord Mayor and officers from the armed forces. The couple had previously visited the city in 1913 to a tremendous reception with thousands lining the city streets to cheer them on. Few could have imagined what the next few years might bring, although there were warning signs in the Balkans with uprisings and the subsequent assassination of Archduke Ferdinand.

The depression of the 1930s saw street disruptions and clashes with the police as unemployment rose to over three million. Manchester was no exception and militant groups formed to voice their opposition to government policies and demand change. The politicians went some way to offering hope, whilst cracking down on any disruptive elements. It was at this time that the Prince of Wales was touring the country in an effort to understand the publics situation and offer any support he could through occupational schemes set-up to alleviate the immediate problems. The prince gained popularity for this 'personal touch' albeit that popularity soon waned as he chose to abdicate the throne in favour of his love for the American, Wallace Simpson.

A smiling Queen Mother greets the crowds in Manchester in the late 1940s and is flanked by King George VI in his RAF Uniform. It looks a happy occasion with the cheering children waving their union flags and the Lord Mayor in his fine ermine hoping not to upstage the Queen Mother. Today the smart phones would be out taking endless photos and videos of everything that happened but all we can see in that respect in the photo is the lady over by the building wall, winding up her 'Kodak Box Brownie' camera to take another snap.

The bombings of Christmas 1940 took their toll on Manchester and just a month later, the Queen Mother and King George VI had paid the city a visit to see the devastation for themselves. It was the Queen Mother asking the questions as her nervous husband surveyed the scene at the Royal Exchange, together with the Home Secretary at the time, Herbert Morrison. The visit was a secret one, given the ongoing war situation, although a few locals had spotted the royals and dignitaries and thought they would view the spectacle from close range.

Some of the Queens duties required her to visit and open exhibitions and these could range from fashion to electrical goods as we see here in Manchester in the late 1950s. The queen looked intrigued by the dishwasher which was being exhibited and at the time was seen as a 'new fangled' kitchen edition from the US. Most families in Manchester would still not have conceived that such a thing could takeover from washing dirty pots in the kitchen sink with 'Fairy Liquid' and it would be at least another 15 years or more until dishwashers began to make their mark in households around Manchester.

It wasn't just culture and industry which were awarded royal visits in Manchester, Queen Elizabeth has a great love of youth and education. Here we see her majesty showing a great interest in the boys art class at Manchester Grammar School in 1965. The school goes all the way back to 1516 when the Bishop of Exeter paid £5 to buy a piece of land near the river to build a school. The Queen would have been aware of this long heritage and also of the many 'Old Mancunians' she would have knighted or given OBE's or MBE's to over the years.

Right: The Princes' love of flying helped him make the easy choice when asked to open Terminal One at Manchester airport in 1962. The crowds were delighted to see royalty once more and another sunny day provided a grand spectacle for the opening ceremony. It was officially opened in 1938 and known as Ringway Airport, named after a small village just south of the airport. Terminal I is the largest of the terminals and has helped the airport become the third busiest airport in the UK, with almost 28 million passengers using the airport in 2017.

Above: Prince Phillip was able to fly a Royal Navy helicopter in to Platt Fields in 1959, as he had already achieved his pilots wings with the RAF in 1953 and in 1956 he also gained helicopter wings. It was a calm and sunny day in Manchester as the Prince headed off to the university to open up two new halls of residence. He was very much the outgoing man of the times and loved excitement and sport. His aide just behind him was trying to catch-up to handover the princes' hat, once the helicopter blades had stopped of course.

MANCHESTER

Below: A major entrepreneurial Manchester business, set-up in the 1980s was 'Joe Bloggs' a jeans and clothing manufacturer. Initially, it attracted much attention on the fashion scene as its reputation for fashionable 'baggy' clothing grew, alongside the new Manchester music scene. A number of dignitaries visited the premises and its founder, Shami Ahmed, but probably none more important than Princess Anne. Shami Ahmed has the visitors book open for the royal signature and no doubt Princess Anne would duly oblige. The company's popularity waned as the music scene changed and the brand went out of fashion, eventually leading to the bankruptcy of its founder, a sad end to an iconic Manchester company.

Left: The prince was only 25 years old when this photo of him, leaving the Town Hall, was captured in 1974. He was already a seasoned officer in the Royal Navy and a helicopter pilot like his father before him. His then smart suits and easy style had endeared him to the public and as such he was warmly welcomed at the Kelloggs factory which he visited later. The smiling dignataries around him would accompany him on the day's visits and ensure the whole day went without any security issues as concerns were running high after the attempted kidnapping of his sister, Princess Anne, by a crazed gunman some months earlier.

Above: Manchester Grammar was lucky enough to receive another royal visit when it hosted Prince Charles and these budding 'potters' clearly enjoyed their conversation with the prince. The Prince of Wales was a great supporter of Grammar Schools and had referenced the benefits on numerous occasions, much to the disdain of those supporting the comprehensive education movement. The prince consolidated his support of Manchester Grammar School when the Prince of Wales Trust became patron of the school in 1998.

SURROUNDING AREAS

This photo was taken just after the turn of the last century around 1910 and although it looks like the long and distant past, there is still at least one building which is clearly recognisable today. The building on the right, was at the time was a bank, as it is today, but now the Royal Bank of Scotland. The scene is the tram terminus on Palatine Road, Didsbury, at the junction with Lapwing Lane. Passengers alight from the trams and meander along the road around the terminal. The fashion of the time is in evidence with ladies in long dresses, together with gents in full three piece suits and hats, The trams of today, operate from the Metrolink which is directly behind where the photographer stood to take this picture all those years ago. To the left, just out of shot, is The Greenfinch pub, situated in a grand old Victorian mansion.

This is a much changed scene today, the wide expanse of road with houses and shops on either side, is very difficult to place on today's busy Cheetham Hill Road, in the outskirts of Manchester. Even with the large church spire to the left and the distinctly pointed roofs of the houses it doesn't give enough clues to the exact location. It is however a classic nostalgic photo of its time, the various forms of transport and with the fashion dress of the two ladies in long skirts, cycling along the cobbles. The boy to the right holds his bike and has clearly spotted the photographer. A 'top hatted' gent in the horse and cart must be going somewhere posh as this definitely was not regular head gear during the day. Trams make their way along the road with not too much else to obstruct their path, which would obviously be much different today on this busy road.

This early 1920s photo of Carrington shows a car coming towards the photographer, whilst a young girl standing at the gate on the left, smiles across at the cameraman. The house she is outside of has since been demolished, but the chapel next door still exists as 'Corner House The Old Chapel' on the A6144 Manchester Road. The building further along the road on the left is the Windmill Inn, which is very much a locals pub, drawing trade from Carrington and nearby Partington. Until 2007, Shell Chemicals UK operated a major petrochemicals manufacturing complex in Carrington.

Liverpool Road, Patricroft, Eccles just outside the city centre, can be seen in these two photos with a time gap of around ten years. The first taken around 1920 showing the prominent 'Join Eccles Co-op' sign below the clock tower to the right, captures passers by looking in shop windows. Three young girls on the left, push a baby in a typical pram of the time. A horse and cart passes on the opposite side of the road. A notable person to be born in Patricroft was Sir Edwin Alliott Verdon Roe. Born in 1877, as mentioned earlier, he was the first Englishman to make a powered flight in 1908.

The later photo, shows a relatively busy junction on the A57 Liverpool Road, which ran all the way from Church Street, Eccles, to the airport out at Barton. For much of its length it was all shops and a traditional pub on almost every corner. Sir John Moore, the pools tycoon, who built the Littlewoods empire, was born in a pub on Liverpool Road.

Below: It has to be a Vauxhall Victor which is making its way towards us in this photo of Gorton in the early 1960s, as the chap on his motor scooter signals a left turn. The Wilson's pub is no longer there and no doubt had to compete with the one opposite selling the popular 'Jubilee Stout'. Many of the buildings have disappeared over time but Gorton remains much the same.

The popular television series 'Shameless' which aired on Channel 4, was mainly filmed in West Gorton Street. The parade of shops used for filming the initial scenes was built on the site of St Mark's Church, Clowes Street, the birthplace of Manchester City F.C.

Right: Shaw Heath roundabout in the early 1960s, with Castle Street and Mercian Way off to the left. The scene is not dissimilar to what you would see today if you took a photograph from outside what was, The Swan public house and near to The Armoury pub.The bank building in the photo on the other side of the roundabout remains, but is now disused. Buildings to the right of the bank are now demolished with 'Our Lady's Primary School' in its place. A man in a flat cap stands on the traffic island admiring the popular vehicles passing by. At the time, the new Singer Gazelle would have been a plusher model the mainstream Hillman Minx.The Gazelle was the first Singer to be produced following the take-over of the Singer company by the Rootes Group in 1956.

Above: Although the shop names and businesses have changed on Ashley Road, Hale, the buildings are still wholly recognisable. Westminster Bank on the left had changed to the NatWest Bank and only recently closed its doors. Much further along in the background, we can see St Peters Church, at the corner of Harrop Road and Ashley Road. This late Victorian church, which was founded in 1892. Today, the street still has the same feel to it, however the type of businesses may have changed and the convertible Bond Minicar Mark G Tourer might look a bit out of place outside Costa Coffee and an M&S Foodhall.

Above: A little way out of the Manchester centre, Failsworth is a small conurbation on the A62 just east of the river. Its name originates from two words of Old English, fegels and worth, meaning 'an enclosure with special fence' and the first mention of it is in records from 1212 AD. Farming, weaving and later, cotton manufacture were its main industries. The landmark on the corner is the Failsworth Pole, erected in 1924, standing proudly on the corner of Pole Lane and Oldham Road. This photograph was taken in the 1950s and The Royal Oak remains a popular venue for locals and others and is a handy drop-in point for bus passengers as the bus stop still exists, just outside of the Church of St John the Evangelist.

Left: Northenden Road, Sale at the turn of the last century is not that different a scene to today's busy thoroughfare. The photographer, would be standing outside what is now Barclays Bank, on the left. The trees have certainly grown and matured in the last hundred years, but there are still shops lining the street on both sides. Undoubtedly, they will be different types of business on the high street and probably include more restaurants, sandwich and cake shops, a bookmaker and a Wetherspoons pub. The church and its spire, to the left in this photo, have long since gone and have been replaced with more modern red brick offices. The horse and cart have been replaced by modern vehicles and a limited amount of on street parking.

Right: This photograph taken on Regent Street looking across the roundabout to Church Street, has changed dramatically since it was taken. Although the buildings on the right remain in tact, the roundabout has gone and the left of the image has changed to the Metro Eccles Interchange. The large building to the right was National Provincial Bank and is now a Solicitors, with the Halifax Building Society next door. The clock tower in the distance belongs to Eccles Town Hall, the municipal building designed by John Lowe and built 1880–81. Just as striking is the Town Hall Tavern, black and white, next to it on the left.

Below: There are still many shops along either side of Moston Lane, but the shop awnings have long since gone. The position of the photographer in this 1950s photo, was just beyond Moston Lane School, opposite Winston Road. The shop awnings and daily shop were a feature of this time as refrigerators were only just becoming available to working households, so goods were protected against the sun and mothers had to shop daily to ensure fresh food was bought for meals.In Moston, the area around Belgrave Road is known to local residents as the "White Stuff" or the "White Hills", in reference to the brickworks' waste that formed steep and unstable hills alongside the brook. These hills were reprofiled during landscaping works carried out in the early 1980s.

WHEN WE WERE YOUNG

You may be able to work out from the photo that this is no production line. There are a variety of activities being carried out by these boys at Alsthoms predecessor company GEC in 1945 with hacksaws, files, chisels and lathes all being used. This is in fact a group of apprentices learning their trade at the training school. There is not much safety gear on view so extra care would be needed to avoid damaging fingers or catching a spur of metal in the eye. Safety would become much more important in later decades as workplace practices were scrutinised by union officials and safety reps. No doubt these chaps would go on to work for many years in the GEC and later, Alsthom workshops of the future.

Right: What to do with a window cleaners cart now that he'd taken off his wooden ladders and buckets to go about his work. On the cobbled back streets of Manchester there was always something to use as a prop or make into a game. Televisions were only just coming into fashion and many of these red bricked terraced houses would not yet have the money to afford one. But these two may have seen John Wayne in a cowboy movie at a friends house or at the Saturday morning picture show and be imagining themselves in a circle of wagons fighting off 'red indians' as they were then called. The cheeky lad on the left, looks like he may have both his thumbs in his ears and wiggling his hands at the camera man in a mischievous way. The window cleaner would be back soon and want his cart back, and if this lad was as cheeky to him, he might just get a 'clip 'round the ear'!

Left: We all have strong memories of our first few days at primary school, although nowadays most children tend to go to pre-school, so it is not such a shock to the system for them as it was for the children of the 1960s! In the 1960s there were no state pre-schools or nurseries, so for most children just turning 5 years old, their first day at school was the first time they had been on their own, away from home. Consequently the first day of school was a very tearful event for both child and parent! Having got over the first pangs of separation, school life soon fell into a predictable routine. School milk was part of this routine.. In Post War Britain school milk, a third of a pint per child, was introduced in schools to supplement the child's diet. In 1971 school milk for the over-sevens was withdrawn by Margaret Thatcher, then Secretary of State for Education – for this she was dubbed 'Thatcher, Thatcher, Milk Snatcher' in the press.

Right: Who needs roundabouts and swings when you have an old chair and some bricks to play with. Fun could be found anywhere when kids are left to play and these five are no exception. On a sunny day in 1962 on a back street in Hulme it was a matter of making up your own games which might include, 'knock-a-door run', 'stick and stone' or marbles, if anyone had any. They were simple pleasures and it didn't matter if you got dirty, as a quick brush down would do the trick. It wouldn't be much longer before this group would be moved, with their families, to the likes of Wythenshaw, Hyde, Worlsey or Heywood as new estates were built to provide modern housing and facilities for the growing populations of the Manchester suburbs.

Above: During the months of September and October, a favourite playground game is conkers. It is a game which has been played every autumn for generations but nowadays fewer children are playing it. On finding your first conker of the season, you should say: " Oddly oddly onker my first conker". This ensures good fortune and few tangles throughout the coming season. A conker is the seed of the horse chestnut tree and the best conkers to play with are uncracked, firm and symmetrical. Each player has a conker hanging on its string. Players take turns at hitting their opponent's conker, as we can see in this photograph taken at Victoria Park in 1974. The game goes on in turns until one or other of the two conkers is completely destroyed.

There's nothing better to trigger a sense of nostalgia than the chimes of an ice cream van. We might live in a world of new-fangled mobile phones, tablets you don't swallow and 4K TV sets that could literally cost you 4K in cash. For the ultimate quality of life, though, all you need is to hear a blast of Greensleeves and then rush out into the fresh air to buy yourself an ice cream. Just like you used to do in the good old days when streets had cobbles and children wore shorts to show off the scabs on their knees! Motorised ice cream vans began to grow in popularity in the 1950. Thinking back to the 1960s, it can be fun to ask people if they are fans of The Beatles or The Rolling Stones. But, when it comes to ice cream, asking for a personal preference is even more of a test of good taste. Are you a Mr Whippy or a Mr Softee? Chocolate, mint, strawberry or vanilla? Raspberry sauce or chocolate sauce? Do you willingly pay extra for a 99 (chocolate Flake) – or would you prefer a scattering of hundreds and thousands?

It was a sunny day in 1955 as we see these youngsters, lads without their shirts of course, exiting the wide mouth of Willie the Whale at the Children's Amusement Park at Belle Vue. The summer frocks of the two girls would be comfortable in the hot sun, whilst the lads in shorts were up for running over to the Helter Skelter or Miniature Railway. Willie the Whale was an innovative idea, as at over 32 feet in length and eight feet high, it housed a small aquarium inside its 'stomach', maybe to symbolise what Willie may have swallowed up, for those who weren't aware of the blue whales plankton diet. Another attraction at the park was the Big Dipper, known as the 'Bobs', a frightening ride which reached immense heights and stomach churning lows. A student named Vance Tutton conquered the ride, reaching a record 325 successive circuits, we have to wonder how he was afterwards though!

M
14
S
MANCHESTER CENTRAL

It was a quiet day in 1955 at Central Station in Manchester and this lad would have been waiting a long time to capture engine numbers for his train spotting album. Before the Beeching cuts of the mid 1960's the railways were everywhere, so it was not uncommon for anyone to live fairly close to a railway line. Trainspotting was one of the most popular hobbies among young boys who would crowd the ends of platforms at the station to record steam engine number's in their Ian Allen books. In this case, the smartly dressed young man in his Sunday best looks as though he has been asked to pose for the photograph. Central Station was a major hub for Manchester, completed in 1880, together with its 210 feet of roof span, it was a magnificent entrance to Manchester for many visitors. Sadly, by the time this young man would have reached his 21st birthday, the station was closed. However, we can still see this iconic Grade II* listed building standing proud as the GMex Center, opened in 1986.

A WOMANS WORK...

The origin of the proverb 'a woman's work is never done' means that a woman often worked longer hours than a man because the housework and raising children are jobs that never end.

This wonderful photo was taken in 1917 as the war continued into its fourth year. With many of Britain's men folk having enlisted in the forces it was women who took up the occupations which had to continue to ensure the country did not come to a grinding halt. Here we have the Station Mistress and her two porters at Irlams O'th Height Station on the Atherton Line, between Pendlebury and Pendleton. The station was opened in 1901 and differed from others in that the platform and building were made completely of wooden planks, rather than the yellow brick common to other stations. The station closed in 1956, but with the distinction of being solely run by women through the first world war.

We have seen previously in this book the Alsthom apprenticed boys at work in their own workshop. Now we see the women of 1927, having moved into the previously male oriented engineering world, in their own workshop at Alsthom. On closer inspection it looks as though these women are engaged in the 'motor windings' section which required delicate and precise work, winding copper wires around magnetic cores which then needed to be insulated, by tradition, in copper or paper bindings. The war, some ten years prior to this photo, had confirmed the capabilities of women in the general workforce and as can be seen from this photo, few occupations needed to be retained as 'men only'.

Right: A woman's work is never done, was doubly true during the Second World War. When men left these shores for battle, it was their womenfolk who filled the void. They donned overalls, dungarees, boiler suits and drivers' uniforms as they turned lathes, harvested the crops, operated heavy machinery and drove lorries. These women worked in an ordnance factory, turning out shell caps. Every so often they would mark one with a message, such as 'this one's for you Adolf' or something a bit fruitier. Women not only saw this work as 'doing their bit' for the war effort, but as a chance to get away from the kitchen sink and rid themselves of the stereotype of existing purely as a baby factory, cook and cleaner. After the war, many women were not prepared to abandon the jobs and careers they had committed themselves to for up to six years. Those men who could not accept that changes had come while they had been away found themselves in dispute with those same loved ones for whom they had been fighting.

Above: The teaching of science to girls is not a new thing as many would have us believe. At the Manchester High School for Girls there was a long tradition of encouraging girls to take part in the wider subjects to broaden their minds and realise that, at such a time for the liberation of women, young girls 'had a duty' to expand themselves in all areas of life. This photo was taken at the school in 1899 in a science lesson. These girls look very interested in their teachers class, although it is difficult to determine what aspect of science they were considering, given the bell jars and test tubes on the bench although they do appear to be inspecting small frogs, one in each jar and one in the teachers hand. What ever the specific subject it was certain that the objectives of the school, founded only 25 years before this photo, would be upheld- 'to impart to girls the very best education which can be given to them for any future which may be before them'.

Below right: At the time the health visiting profession began, living conditions for the urban poor were often cramped and extremely insanitary, leading to many business owners sending women around to workers' homes to educate their wives about sanitation and nutrition. The initial focus of health visiting was on families with young children. In 1929, health visitors began to be employed by local councils on a statutory basis and since 1974 they have been employed by the National Health Service. We can see from this staged photograph how clean and tidy the antenatal clinic was back in the 1930s.

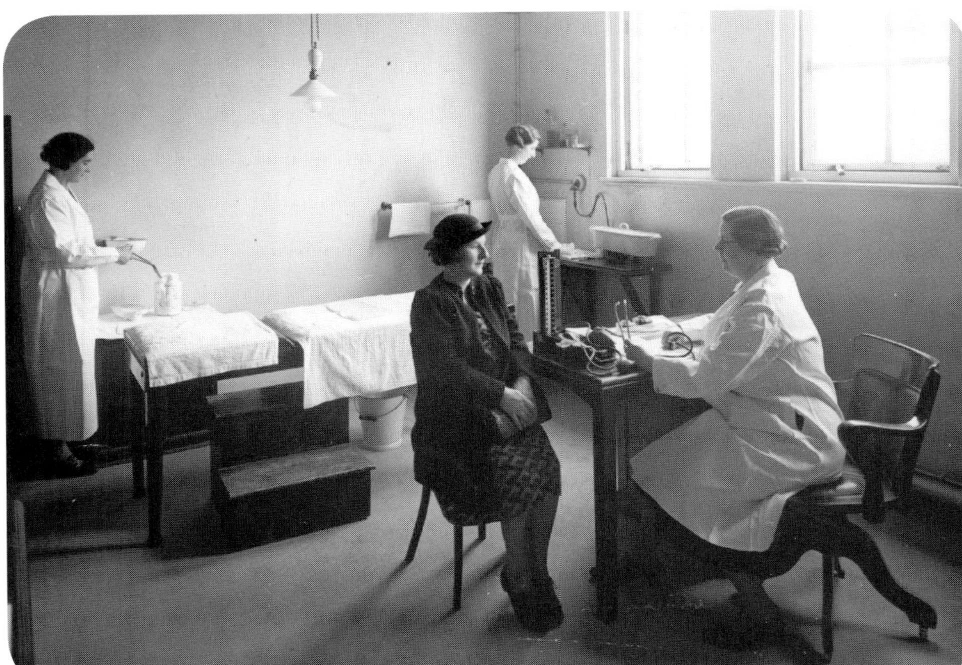

The more traditional roles for women in the workplace of course still continued and the administrative, filing and typing occupations were at the time considered to be more diligently carried out by women. This was most definitely the case in 1933 at JD Williams of Manchester. The early 'mail order' company was based in Dale Street and at Princess Street and maybe its type of operations and main customers suited a female centred workforce as many of its products were under clothing and garments. Their publication 'Buyers Guide to Shopping' could be recognised as one of the first mail order catalogues in the UK and with its slogan 'This is our only salesman' would have laid the way for much bigger mail order firms such as Littlewoods, Grattans and Argos.

Below: Two fabulous models show off Evening Gowns of the Lancashire fabric, "Grafton's Meronelle," in, Manchester, November 1931.Vintage style evening dresses tended to be fitted in the waist, easing out mid-thigh, where they flared elegantly to the floor. There were gowns with puffs and ruffle sleeves, and later in the decade high necks and halter styles with plunging backs were in fashion. Silky, clinging fabrics were common in evening gowns, often worn with a fur. Fabrics that were popular included chiffon, silk, crepe-de-chines, and satin. Evening dresses had hems that very nearly touched the floor and often had small trains in the back.In the 1930s, short hair was in style, women attempted to cheer themselves up with pampering in the form of beauty products and hairstyling. Weekly visits to the salon were in order to set hair in the latest fingers waves and tight rolls.

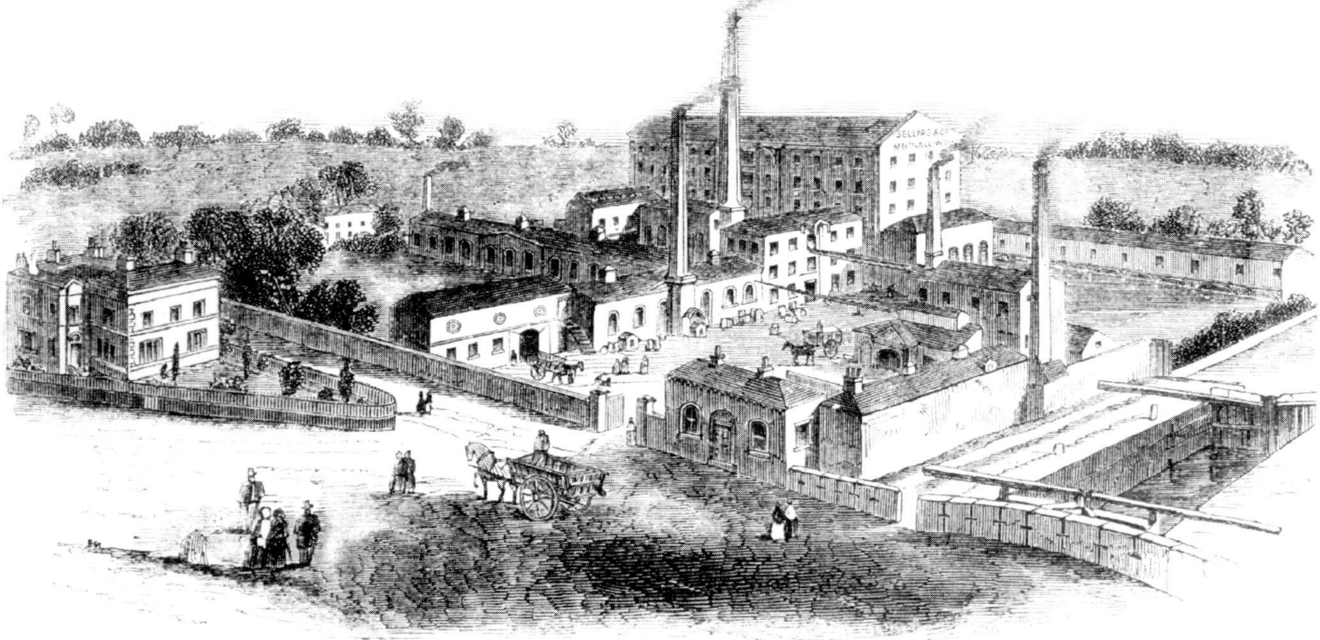

Elcometer

Providing inspection equipment solutions across the globe

For 200 years the enterprising Sellars family have set up and run businesses around Manchester, identifying new opportunities and meeting the demand for innovative solutions.

The family business journey started with soap and starch and eventually diversed into Elcometer Ltd, which is involved in the design, manufacture and supply of inspection equipment for the coatings and concrete sector, industrial metal detectors, and ultrasonic non-destructive testing equipment for corrosion thickness and flaw detection.

Barratt Carrington Sellars started the business in 1818 at Newton Heath. The company was known as Sellars & Co Starch & Soap Manufacturers, and in the mid-1800s changed its name to East Lancashire Chemical Co when it moved to new premises in Droylsden – a move it was compelled to undertake by the authorities as the business had considerably expanded and the fumes from acids etc became a nuisance to the neighbourhood.

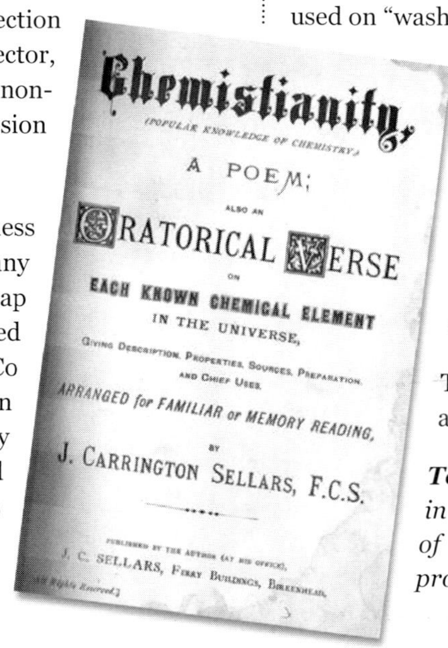

Chemistianity,

(POPULAR KNOWLEDGE OF CHEMISTRY.)

A POEM;

ALSO AN

ORATORICAL VERSE

ON

EACH KNOWN CHEMICAL ELEMENT

IN THE UNIVERSE,

GIVING DESCRIPTION, PROPERTIES, SOURCES, PREPARATION AND CHIEF USES.

ARRANGED for FAMILIAR or MEMORY READING,

BY

J. CARRINGTON SELLARS, F.C.S.

PUBLISHED BY THE AUTHOR (AT HIS OFFICE),

J. C. SELLARS, FERRY BUILDINGS, BIRKENHEAD.

[All Rights Reserved.]

The main products were industrial soap used in the booming factories and washing soda under the ELCO brand name (East Lancashire Chemical Co).

By the 1890s the company was making cement as well as soap. Soda Crystal production began around 1900 and grew into a huge industry as soda crystals and soap were the two main products used on "wash day".

Post-war the business was being run by a John Carrington Sellars and the business climate had changed. Due to the decline in the manufacturing industry and hence the drop in demand for industrial soap, he decided to expand the business into the manufacture of measuring instruments following an opportune meeting in a hardware shop.

The first Elcometer measuring instrument, known as the ELCO Meter (which is still in manufacture

***Top:** The original Sellars & Co Soap Manufactory in Newton Heath, Manchester. **Left:** The cover of a poem book for each known chemical element produced by J. Carrington Sellars.*

today as the Elcometer 101) was built in 1946 and launched the following year priced at £10.50 and the division – which was later to become Elcometer Ltd was up and running.

The first export sale took place the same year with BAMR, a family-owned business in South Africa, the third generation of which are still distributors for Elcometer today.

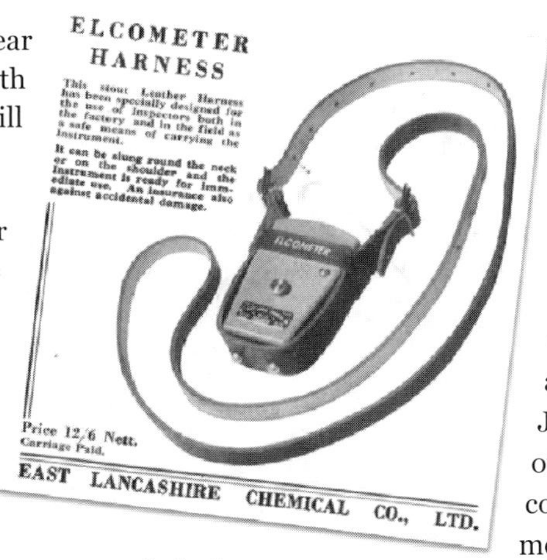

The company developed the first transistor coating thickness gauge and launched the Elcometer 103 Elcotector in 1960.

Following the death of John Carrington Sellars, his sons, Peter and Ian Sellars, took over the business in 1962 and renamed it Elcometer Instruments Ltd. Several innovative products were launched in the succeeding years and in 1978 Elcometer was awarded The Queen's Award for Export.

Ian Carrington Sellars took 100% ownership in 1983 and company growth continued with eight extensions over the years culminating in 1986 with a purpose built production building. The original shop floor became the research and development facility.

The company was now also launching software products and the Queen's Award for Technology was awarded in 1990. The following year the world's first pocket gauge with statistics and memory, The Elcometer 345, was brought to market.

The current managing director, Michael Carrington Sellars – son of Ian – joined the business in 1995, although he was already familiar with his surroundings having spent many of his holidays as a youth working in the family business.

Significant developments in 2003 saw Elcometer purchase Braive Instruments and its company Braive France Sarl – leading manufacturers of physical test equipment to the paint and powder industry. The companies became part of the Elcometer worldwide business network. Also purchased that year was Protovale (Oxford) Ltd, the UK's leading manufacturer of concrete inspection equipment which brought an additional range of concrete inspection and metal detection equipment to the product portfolio.

Elcometer was performing well and the future vision was more expansion at home and abroad. In 2007 new headquarters were opened on its current site, doubling the factory space and adding new production, office and training facilities.

The following year Michael Sellars took over the company following the sudden death of his father and the company was renamed Elcometer Ltd.

An American company was bought in 2011 when Elcometer purchased Dakota Ultrasonics Incorporated of Santa Cruz, California which designed and manufactured a comprehensive range of ultrasonic NDT corrosion thickness and flaw detectors. It was a busy year with a new office also opening in Japan and the launch of the next generation of the best-selling Elcometer 456 gauges with colour screen, accelerometer and alpha-numeric memory.

Top left: *Mr Ian Sellars, 1980.* ***Left:*** *Early advertising for the 'Elcometer' Inspector Harness.* ***Below:*** *Elcometer's 50th Anniversary. H.R.H. The Duke of Kent with Mr Ian Sellars.*

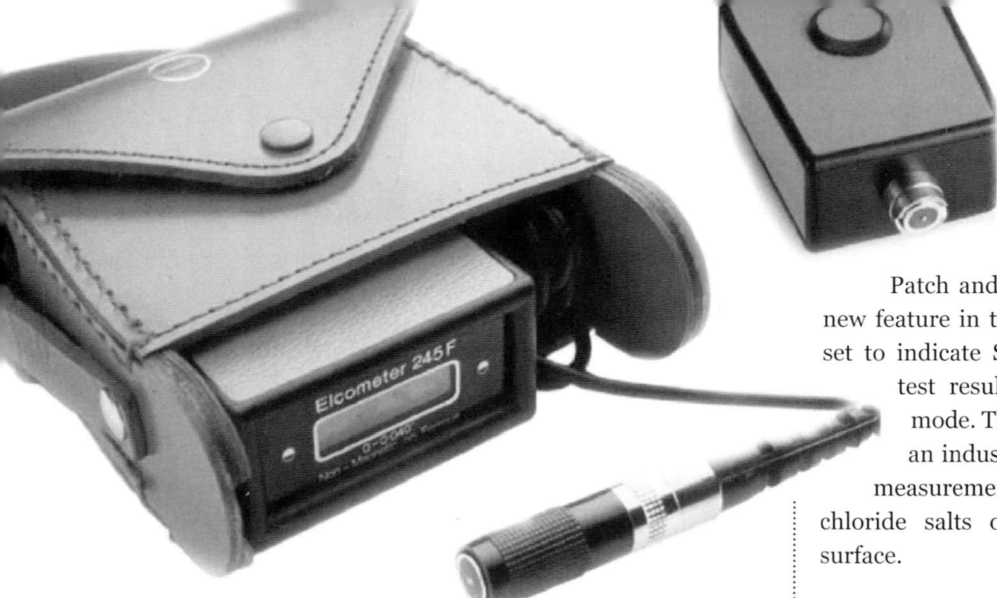

the presence of soluble sodium chloride salts on pre-coated surfaces. Research and development work by Elcometer has established equivalence of the two Bresle Patch and Saturated Filter Paper Methods. This led to a new feature in the latest Elcometer130SSP gauge which can be set to indicate Saturated Filter Paper salt test results in Bresle equivalent mode. The new gauge represents an industry breakthrough in the measurement of soluble sodium chloride salts on a pre-coated surface.

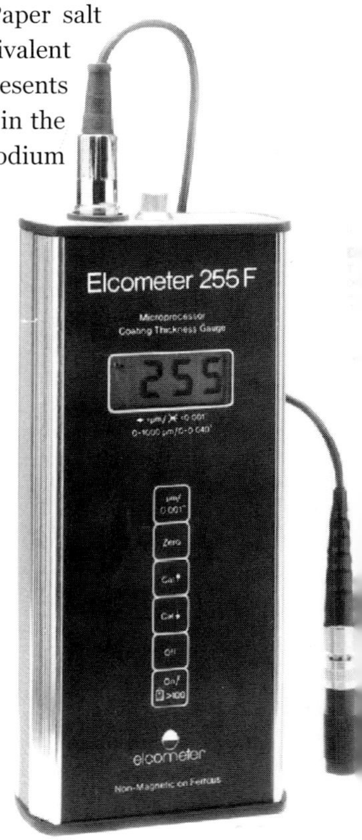

More ground-breaking innovation from Elcometer has led the US Navy to amend its coating specifications following two US Navy sponsored projects. The first was a National Shipbuilding Research Program commission in which four private shipyards performed side-by-side dry film thickness testing (DFT) using the Elcometer 456 with Ultra/Scan Probe and the New Elcometer 456 Industrial Protective Coating (IPC) Gauge. These Elcometer gauges and the industry changing test methods that they represent, were compared with the current US Navy specified test method for DFT measurement.

The Manchester site was further expanded again the following year and a new office opened in Houston, Texas, in 2014.

The next acquisition came in 2016 with Blastline Ltd, designers and manufacturers of portable blast machines. To accommodate the new product range, the adjoining site on Crabtree Lane was bought which almost doubled the available floor space to 115,500 sq ft. In 2017 new offices were opened in Dubai, UAE, trading as EL Inspection & Blasting Equipment LLC. To further accommodate the new range of blast machines and the distribution of those products within Europe, Elcometer opened a second sales and distribution facility in Leer, Germany.

Elcometer had spread far and wide since developing its first measuring instrument and to celebrate its 70th year in 2017 it held a World Sales Conference attended by 80 distributors from 43 countries around the world. It was an opportunity for interested parties to come together and learn about up-to-date options in their specialised fields and future developments.

For instance, Elcometer is seeing the coatings market transitioning itself to provide more complex solutions beyond just paint, with the use of complex substrates, software and intelligent coatings now being the norm. Likewise, Elcometer's software and recording capabilities offer key solutions to ease site maintenance and speedier inspection reporting making it a key partner for forward-thinking companies.

Another recent development involves the measurement techniques used to understand

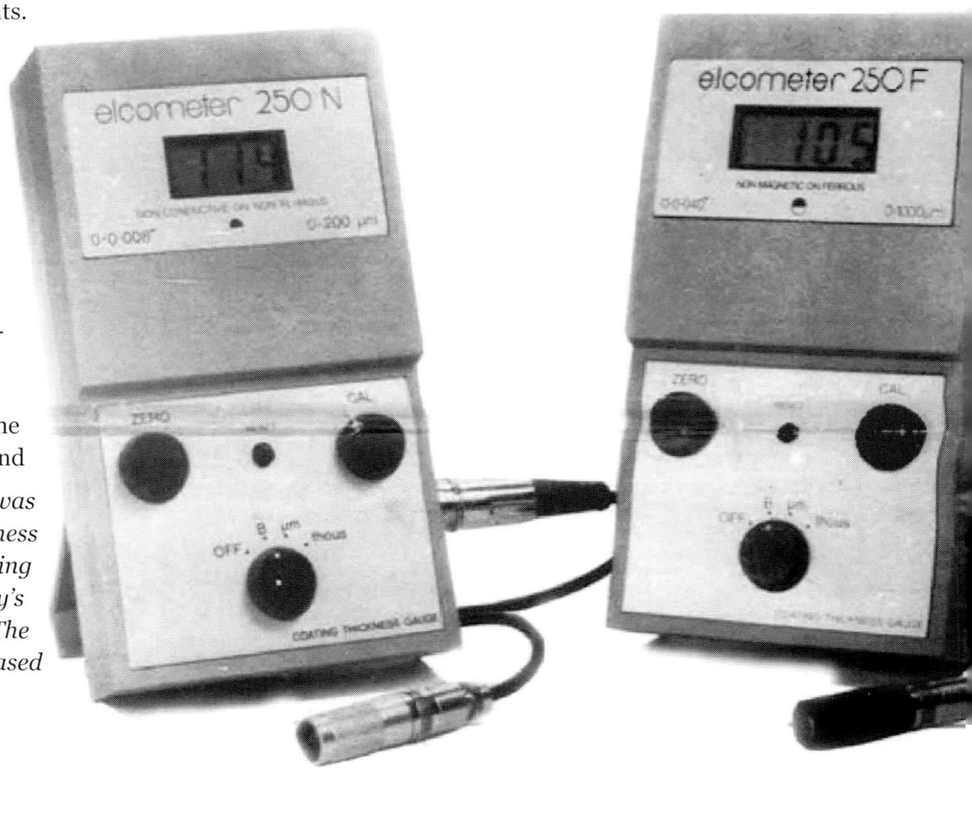

***Top left:** Elcometer's 245F which at the time was the world's smallest, solid state coating thickness gauge for paint, electroplating, galvanising and metal coatings. **Right:** The company's 250 series of the early 1980s. **Top right:** The Elcometer 255 Hand Held Microprocessor Based Digital Coating Thickness Gauge.*

Spectacular results followed with the Ultra/Scan probe and IPC completing inspections in a fraction of the time and with greater precision that the US Navy's referenced test method. A follow-up study performed by the Naval Research Laboratory and Vision Point Systems in which findings from the shipyard study were replicated using the latest application and analytical tools in a rigorously controlled laboratory environment.

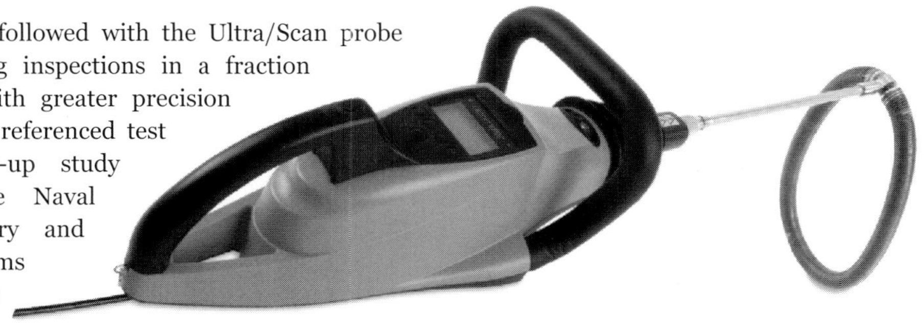

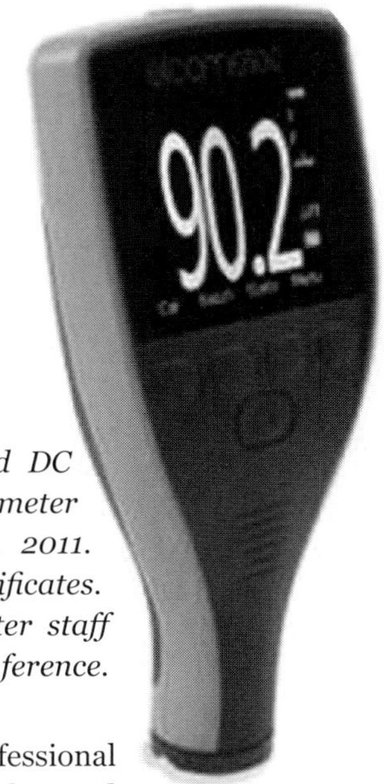

Above: *The Elcometer 280 Pulsed DC Holiday Detector.* ***Right:*** *The Elcometer 456 Integral Gauge, launched in 2011.* ***Below:*** *Elcometer QMA certificates.* ***Bottom:*** *Distributors and Elcometer staff at the World Sales Conference.*

The data from these pioneering research projects were sufficient objective evidence for the US Navy to amend their coating specifications and include the revolutionary technologies contained in both the Ultra/Scan probe and the 456IPC.

Elcometer has also recently made impressive inroads into its gloss measurement range. The company has been supplying glossmeters for more than 40 years, the original product being the Elcometer 401. In 2014 manufacturing of glossmeters was brought in-house and not long afterwards huge development came with the launch of the Elcometer 480. This meter boasts advanced features such batch memory, scanning mode and data output to ElcoMaster. This proved immediately popular and sales of glossmeters soared by 60%. Further improvements are expected as Elcometer continues research and development into the Elcometer 480 and other glossmeters.

An interesting breakthrough which has led to spin-off sales is the time-saving ElcoMaster Data Management Software which has transformed inspection reporting. Elcometer was one of the first in the industry to develop such software. ElcoMaster was established when the PC market was booming and there was increased demand for professional inspectors. The need for gauges with batch memory was increasing as businesses were pushing for more inspection reports in a paperless environment.

ElcoMaster was the perfect solution, cutting down inspection time as reports were now completed in seconds. No longer was there a need to write measurements down with a pen and paper as all data is uploaded onto a PC and turned into professional reports at the click of a button. ElcoMaster was then developed into an app for Android smartphones and eventually iPhones with the app now having a bar code input. This all makes ElcoMaster a game-changer and there is no equivalent platform on the market. It can be downloaded free of charge and once a customer has a positive experience using

Below: Michael Sellars, Managing Director speaking at the Elcometer World Sales Conference. ***Above:*** *Celebrating 70 years of Elcometer with staff and distributors at the company's new Crabtree facility.* ***Opposite page:*** *The Elcometer Head Quarters.*

the software, sales of other Elcometer gauges that are compatible with ElcoMaster follow.

All Elcometer products are designed to comply with national and international standards and the company works with various bodies around the world to ensure its products are fit for purpose and exceed the demands of customers. For example, Elcometer works closely with the Society for Protective Coatings (SSPC) which has developed and published over 100 standards for surface preparation and the application and inspection of protective coatings in the industrial protective coatings markets.

Four core values are at the heart of Elcometer quality – Pride, Ownership, Focus and Initiative – with all employees encouraged to identify improvement opportunities. Previously, quality management systems focused on quality assurance, but as the complexity of the business and its products evolved, it has been recognised that there is a need for change. Work has started on enhancing management systems and processes to include more quality control, develop the organisation's capabilities, introduce cost of quality measures to drive improvement projects and plan for future needs with a roadmap for the quality function.

Communicating well with customers is a vital part of building good relationships and the business has taken advantage of the technology available today with that aim. The Elcometer YouTube channel has grown dramatically and features dozens of product videos including "how to" videos on products such as viscosity flow cups and the Elcometer 500. Subtitles are available in 20 different languages and are popular all over the world.

Exports account for 90% of all sales through more than 80 distributors and offices in France, Belgium, The Netherlands, Germany, Singapore, Japan, the USA and the UAE. The export team has fluency in several languages including Spanish, German, French and Ukrainian. Elcometer also provides customers

with a broad distributor network so they can access Elcometer products wherever they are in the world without difficulty.

Innovation is constant and successful and in the last 10 years more than 100 models have been launched ranging from adhesion products to climate gauges. A highly-skilled production workforce builds and assembles the majority of key products. As a responsible company, Elcometer takes its green responsibilities seriously and is committed to reducing its impact on the environment, including product manufacture, packaging, catalogue production and waste management. All products are lead and mercury free.

Continued growth and demand for Elcometer inspection equipment has recently resulted in the need for further expansion of the Netherlands' and Dubai offices. By increasing the amount of space in its existing building, Elcometer BV tripled their sales and marketing office space, and EL Inspection & Blasting Equipment LLC moved to a new and larger building. Elcometer also open their new ISO 9001 registered Northern American Headquarters in autumn 2018, tripling the site and providing a training and demonstration centre as well as sales, service and technical support.

Michael Sellars said the business had witnessed incredible growth even with global financial crashes, oil prices dropping and cyclical industrial trends. This had been possible through innovation in research and development, investing in the workforce and concentrating on maintaining the existing product ranges whilst improving their quality and productivity.

Greater Manchester Funeral Service Ltd

Caring for families through their difficult times

For over 30 years Michael Kennedy has been helping grieving families through the most difficult times of their lives.

As a respected funeral director his caring attitude coupled with an understanding nature has seen many hundreds of families turn to him for help as they are left carrying the burden of stress following the loss of a loved one.

It's a difficult profession in which to operate, but one that has proved a suitable fit for Mr Kennedy who has had to overcome personal obstacles over the years to set up the Greater Manchester Funeral Service Ltd.

He was brought up a Catholic and went into a seminary, aged 17, to become a secular Catholic priest, but later felt God wanted him to take another path in life and started working in 1983 at Leech's Funeral Service, Moss Side, Manchester as a casual driver.

***Above:** Greater Manchester Funeral Services offices on Moston Lane, Manchester.* ***Below left:** Mr Michael Kennedy.*

It was a difficult time for Mr Kennedy as his parish priest and mentor for the last 6 years passed away – he was the main reason Mr Kennedy entered the seminary. Frustrated with his driving duties at Leech's he began to enquire about opening his own funeral business, much to the annoyance of his employers.

Then, in November 1984, a twist of fate put him on a path to realizing his ambition.

There was a fire in a mill close to his home in Ancoats, Manchester. Mr Kennedy was passing at the time and noticed it was full of evening workers who were unaware of the fire engulfing the stairwell and side entrance of the mill. He ran over and set off the fire alarm and fortunately everyone escaped the building before it was engulfed in flames. The media reported the incident as the "worst fire seen in Manchester since the blitz." A few days later Mr Kennedy was dismissed from his driving role at Leech's which he says was prompted by his ambitions of owning his own funeral business.

Not long afterwards in 1985 he was approached by a millionaire businessman who had read Mr Kennedy's story in the Manchester Evening News and said he was interested in becoming an investor in his potential funeral service.

With an investor on board Mr Kennedy was able to plan for the future and take the plunge. He set up the Kennedy's Funeral Service on Oldham Road, Ancoats, which opened in April 1986, and business flourished.

Visitors reception area.

But, like in all areas of business, problems are never far away and Mr Kennedy, regrettably, had to sell up due to ill health. Many difficult court cases followed in respect of restriction clauses and other legalities as he aimed to return to the profession. Kennedy's Funeral Service was followed by MK Funerals and Michael Kennedy's Funeral Service serving the bereaved families of Collyhurst, Moston and Blackley up until February 2011, when due to both his parents' health problems worsening, he had no alternative than to sell off his company and family trading name, Kennedy, to care for them both.

Sadly, they both passed away within four months of each other in 2012 and he then decided to take a sabbatical from the funeral business. In 2014 he was back running an independent family business, this time known as the Greater Manchester Funeral Service in Moston, based at "Kennedy House" in Moston Lane. His two sons, Michael and Alfie, now work alongside him, as do his sister-in-law Julie, his cousin Catherine, and several long serving employees from his old companies who have again reunited with Mr Kennedy.

Above: *A traditional black horse drawn carriage hearse.*

Back in the 19th century Victorian England, bright colours were unheard of. Back then, the mourning process was rigidly governed by convention especially for the better off families. Clocks in a house would be stopped at the time of death, mirrors were draped or turned to the wall, and curtains were drawn. The length of time for mourning appropriate for a widow or widower, a child or parent, was clearly spelt out. Deep mourning for a widow might be two years, followed by a period of half-mourning. Within that timescale, codes of dress, especially for women were quite detailed as were what was and was not appropriate activity.

Men, who had to continue with their working lives, were less bound by convention, but they too had to adhere to the appropriate dress

Consultation Room.

St Johns chapel.

Chapel of the Holy Family.

***Above:** An example of Greater Manchester Funeral Services white horse drawn carriage hearse.* ***Below:** We have a close relationship with many local florists to supply a wide range of floral tributes.*

and behavior expected from them for their place in the family. Death in the poorer classes involved fewer rituals and that was seen as a lack of respectability by the better off.

A long-standing tradition which is still popular today is the funeral procession which is led by the hearse, containing the coffin and funeral flowers, followed by the limousine driving immediate family of the deceased.

A full service of care and options is provided by the experienced staff which includes the emotional support and practical advice which is so important.

Liaising with the relevant authorities, cemeteries, crematoriums, doctors and clergy, is carried out on the mourners' behalf by the Kennedy family which prides itself of helping other families through their grief every step of the way.

Not all funerals are just family affairs though. Occasionally, there is widespread interest and the most high-profile funeral Mr Kennedy recalls conducting was that of the late Pauline Reade in 1987, the last victim to be found following the Moors Murders by Ian Brady and Myra Hindley, who killed five children around Manchester in the 1960s and whose crimes shocked the world. Pauline, aged 16, was a neighbour of Hindley and was the first victim. She was abducted on her way to a dance in Gorton, Manchester, in July, 1963.

Additional services sometimes requested include a horse drawn carriage hearse, floral tributes, monumental headstones and additional inscriptions, releasing of doves, press announcements, preneed funeral plans, catering (at home or public location), loan bagpiper, solo singers, memorial booklets, jazz bands, probate solicitors and assistance with flights or ferry transfers.

Over his long career in the profession, Mr Kennedy Dip NAFD, MBIFD CFSMA, has seen many changes, some favourable, some not, but he accepts that in all walks of life change is inevitable. "The changes have been in some way upsetting with old traditions no longer continued. The younger generation do not look on religion as an important part of living and dying.

Church services have become less popular and increasingly it's straight to a crematorium or cemetery chapel with civil celebrants or humanists the norm," he said. There is also a growing trend for families to choose cremations over burial. Mr Kennedy explains: "Graves need to be attended to and visits made to cemeteries regularly, so families choose cremations to keep their personal available time for the enjoyment of life. Having the ashes scattered means one visit a year to that section of the crematorium, or having the ashes at home means there is no need to venture out at all".

The choice of funeral music in the modern age varies from the bizarre to sublime."On occasion we have had the Star Wars theme as the coffin went through for cremation. Monty Python's 'Bright Side of Life' is a popular song also," said Mr Kennedy.

Technology also plays its part as crematoriums now increasingly use a USB port so during the funeral service the life of the deceased can be shown through film to music.

***Above:** We provide addtional inscriptions and restoration to any existing memorials.*

Customer testimonials

Michael is the best there is. A warm compassionate man who goes beyond the realms he has to he ensure everything is done with RESPECT and Dignity. His attention to the bereaved and the person they have lost is without question most attentive and compassionate.

Sadly for myself I have lost two extremely close family members but feel I gave them the best send off when I entrusted them to Michaels care.

His premises are beautiful, spotless and smelled lovely, this was important to me that my loved ones were in the care of such a caring company. All the staff I met were respectful and nothing was to much trouble for them.

From the bottom of my broken heart I thank God that I had Michael in such devastating times. Thank you
BlackDesk63-2

My Grandad had a wonderful send off. Michael Kennedy is a gentleman, all aspects of funeral were arranged in a professional manner. My Grandad looked impeccable. Michael & Karen are kind and considerate, they go above & beyond. The drivers too are so helpful. Thank you to all.
The Ward Family.

This was a devastating time for our family, first our Dad then 18 months later our beloved Nan. Karen Bremmer was a god send. She made everything so easy. Her support was absolutely amazing. All the team here went above and beyond.
Sue. S.

Another growing request is to have horse drawn funerals, but not with black plumes or black drapes but football team flags and colours. Coffins also in a team's colours or themes from the lifestyle of the deceased are also available.

A large selection of coffins and caskets can be chosen at the funeral home in Moston or the family home by arrangement.

Many people today see funerals as a way to celebrate the deceased's life rather than mourn their passing and that view has been a driver in bringing changes to funeral services. With a more mobile population than ever before, the life of a funeral director often takes him or her away from their own patch.

The Greater Manchester Funeral Service Ltd, which operates a 24-hour, 365 days a year personal service, supplies all services involved in repatriation to and from the UK, for example to countries in Europe and across Africa, which includes obtaining all documentation by personally visiting embassies in London to assist the families and prevent further distress.

Julie Kennedy.

Michael Kennedy Jnr.

Alfie Jake Kennedy.

Karen Brammer.

"Let my family help your family"

You are not alone in your loss. My family and I will be here every step of the way, ensuring your requests are treated with discretion, care and professionalism.

We will inform you of everything you have requested in writing and a full breakdown of the funeral charges will be given within hours of the arrangements.

We at Greater Manchester Funeral Services pride ourselves on a full range of services for what is a most difficult and emotional time.

A traditional funeral leaving from your home address would comprise of the following:

- A 24-hours-a-day emergency service for the conveyancing of the deceased from the place of death to our private chapel of rest during business hours.
- Care of the deceased and use of any of our three chapels of rest until the day of the funeral.
- Liaison with clergy, cemetery/crematorium, and consultation with the medical profession or coroners officers in connection with cremation certificates or burial authorisation.
- Our professional attention and guidance during the funeral arrangements.
- The supply of our Clarke veneered oak coffin shown in our brochure, one hearse & pallbearers.
- Your family will receive a 100% personal, caring, dignified funeral service on the funeral day.

The following are not included and can be discussed and added if required:

- Embalming and preparation treatment
- The use of our 7 seater limousines
- Floral Tributes
- A horse drawn carriage (Black or white)
- Catering
- Press notices
- Lone Piper or Jazz band
- Soloist singer or Organist
- The use of our chapel of rest for visiting at weekends or out-of-hours

Above: *We can arrange catering at one of our recommended local establishments. Shown here is The World Irish Heritage Centre in Cheetham, Manchester.*

A more modern development across the funeral industry internationally is pre-need funeral plans which remove a possible financial headache for bereaved families. Also, making funeral arrangements can be very emotional as you are making choices on behalf of a family member and some people are left wondering "did I make the right choice." With pre-need funeral plans the discussion can take place in advance and with the right guidance from the Kennedy family, people can be satisfied the right choices will be made.

The UK is currently lagging behind the rest of Europe when it comes to end-of-life planning with only 6 per cent of adults having taken out a pre-paid funeral plan. It is much more common elsewhere. In Holland for example, 70 per cent of people have a funeral plan and 20 million Spaniards have funeral insurance.

But, whether the world's press turns out for a funeral, or just a handful of mourners, a high level of professional standards remains the goal and Mr Kennedy said for that to happen there needs to be a well trained team working together.

"To have a successful business you need to have good staff, your business is nothing without the team you employ. A happy workforce works well together," he said.

William Hulme's Grammar School, circa 1920.

William Hulme's Grammar School

'The best in everyone'

In times past many of us stayed on at our local school only until the age of just 14 before leaving for the world of work. Other somewhat younger readers may have attended a 'Secondary Modern' or a brand new Comprehensive school. Still others may have passed their 'eleven-plus' and gone to a Grammar School. And some readers will have attended a school which can trace its history back to the Victorian era, and its roots to events which occurred three centuries ago – Manchester's William Hulme's Grammar School.

THE EARLY YEARS

The story begins back in the 17th century with William Hulme (1631-1691) who was the founder of the William Hulme Charity. Very little is known about William's life except that after the death of his father (also called William Hulme) in 1637, Hulme's uncle John acted as his guardian and he was probably educated in Manchester.

Opinions differ as to his adult life, some maintain that he followed a career at Law after attending Brasenose College, Oxford; others believe that he lived the life of a country gentleman. What we do know with certainty is that his marriage in 1653 brought Hulme to an estate and mansion at Kearsley, near Bolton, where he would reside in later life and that he held the position of Justice of the Peace for Kearsley.

Hulme also owned major properties at Hulme Hall (later Broadstone Hall) in Reddish, Withingreave Hall in Withy Grove, Manchester, and Outwood near Prestwich.

The premature and tragic death of his beloved only son was however to deeply affect William Hulme; in later life he was determined to make some charitable provision for young boys.

On his death in 1691, William left an enormous philanthropic bequest. He was buried in Hulme Chapel of the Collegiate Church in Manchester (now Manchester Cathedral), which had been largely built by his ancestors.

WILLIAM'S LEGACY

In his will, William left provision for the foundation of 'exhibitions' or grants for four students to study for Bachelor of Arts degrees at Brasenose College. The income from this charity was originally £64 a year which came from rents and dues on William's many outlying properties at Heaton Norris, Denton, Ashton-under-Lyne, Reddish and Harwood in Greater Manchester.

Over the years, with the growth of Manchester, the value and income from the original Hulme estate grew to such an extent that it became necessary on several occasions to change the scope of his bequest by Act of Parliament. In 1881, the Trustees of the charity were empowered to build schools in Manchester, Oldham and Bury.

The Trustees also founded a Hall of Residence for students at Manchester University, made annual grants to the University itself, and to the Manchester High School for Girls. The exhibitions at Brasenose College were increased from four to twenty.

In 1881 the Trustees agreed to build a new school in Manchester. A site for it was bought off Alexandra Road between Alexandra Park and Wilbraham Road.

At that time Spring Bridge Road was nothing more than a dirty lane petering out on the school site.

***Above:** Early study. **Left:** The first Class in 1887. **Bottom:** An early photograph of the Lacrosse team.*

NEW SCHOOL

The new school was designed to accommodate 400 boys, with ample space for playgrounds, gymnasium and cricket fields. A headmaster, Mr Joseph Hall, was appointed on an annual salary of £150, plus a capitation fee of £2 for every boy admitted to the school.

The school opened on 26 January, 1887, with sixty-four boys. Originally named The Hulme Grammar School, in 1939 it changed its name to William Hulme's Grammar School.

A student named Bernard Muth claimed to be the first pupil to step over the threshold. His devotion to the school would be evidenced by the fact that one of his last appearances at the school, before his death in 1965 at the age of 88, was when he played alongside his grandson in the school orchestra.

***Left:** The School Hall in the 1920s. **Below:** A bird's eye view of the School and playing fields in the mid-1920s.*

Few would ever forget the school's Latin motto 'Fide sed cui vide' - a punning witticism on the founder's name – 'Trust, but in whom take care'.

And if the motto were an insufficient reminder of whose bounty was ultimately behind the school's existence there was also the school prayer:

"O Lord, the resurrection and the life of them that believe, to be praised as well as those that live as in those that are departed: we give thee thanks for William Hulme, of whose bounty this school was founded and endowed, for William Roberts, Edward Donner and others our benefactors, past and present, by whose beneficence we are here maintained for the further attaining of Godliness and learning: beseeching thee to grant that we, well using to thy glory these Thy gifts, may rise again to eternal life with those that are departed in the faith of Christ: through Christ our Lord. Amen."

Down the many decades since the school first opened its doors thousands upon thousands of pupils have received their education at 'William Hulme's' taking away with them at the end of their school days, not only well earned examination certificates, but also memories which last a lifetime.

No-one and nothing can ever erase those memories: teachers loved or hated, school dinners, ink wells and blotting paper; the smells of chalk dust and changing rooms; bad things such as the cane, and good things such as sporting events and academic triumphs. Laughter and tears; friends made for life.

A poignant reminder of this can be seen in the entrance foyer of the main school building, where on the wall there are two bronze plaques of identical design and size, in memory of old boys of the school who died serving their country in the two World Wars.

In more recent times, there have been many prominent visitors to the school. On 25 June, 1993, Her Royal Highness the Princess Royal opened the Zochonis Centre. In addition, the school was delighted to host a visit by their Royal Highnesses the Earl and Countess of Wessex, on Friday 13 May, 2005. Also visiting the school were the Lord Mayor and Mayoress of Manchester, the Vice Lord Lieutenant, the High Sheriff and local MP, the late Sir Gerald Kaufman. This visit, together with a visit from Lord Andrew Adonis, the then Minister of State for Education, was to be the catalyst for William Hulme's making the transition from a selective grammar school to a city academy and was one of the first independent schools to do so.

David Marsden, a former pupil of the school from 1950 to 1958, a School Governor from 1984 and subsequently Chair of Governors from 1999 to the present day and Steve Patriarca, Headmaster from 2000-2008, seized the opportunity offered by the Labour government to create a non-fee paying school for the 21st century.

ENVIABLE REPUTATION

The school is now able to continue in its long tradition of serving Manchester children from all backgrounds. So, 120 years after its foundation, William Hulme's Grammar School took the exciting step of becoming a United Learning Academy in 2007 and since then all of its students have enjoyed the benefits of learning in state-of-the-art facilities whilst being part of a school with a proud history of academic excellence.

The school maintains its enviable reputation for promoting learning beyond the classroom thanks to its 'Star Student' scheme. William Hulme's offers an impressive range of opportunities including the Duke of Edinburgh's Award Scheme, CCF, sports, music and drama activities and a wide variety of other clubs and societies. The House system remains strong and enables students to take part in and enjoy activities in the spirit of healthy competition and friendship. The Houses are named after eminent Mancunians (Byrom, Dalton, Gaskell and Heywood) and date back to the founding of the school.

Under the leadership of Peter Mulholland, the current Principal since 2008, William Hulme's students have continued to achieve excellent results and there are high expectations of all students whatever their background or starting point. The curriculum is designed to allow all students to flourish and succeed. There is a strong emphasis on core subjects such as Maths, English and Science with a range of options that can be tailored to suit all students' needs. Similarly, the pastoral system focuses on challenging and supporting individuals in a safe and disciplined environment.

Above: *The latest new build at the school – the new Primary Phase Building.* ***Below:*** *A Chemistry lesson in 1927.*

STRONG TRADITIONS

The principal Mr Peter Mulholland said, "I am proud that William Hulme's Grammar School is the most popular primary and secondary school in Greater Manchester. It is a unique school, educating children and young people from the age of 3 to 18 on one school site. William Hulme's has a strong tradition as a successful independent school and is now at the forefront of educational change as a United Learning Academy with high aspirations for all our students".

"Our vision for the future at William Hulme's, is that we believe in the 'best in everyone' and aim to achieve this by combining the best of the independent and state sectors. We want to work closely with parents and the wider community in our bid to achieve this ambitious aim".

"William Hulme's prides itself on being a friendly, culturally diverse community that produces happy, successful and active members of society. Whilst we have a very strong academic focus throughout the school, at William Hulme's Grammar School we believe that there is more to a good education. As well as ensuring our students achieve well academically, we also aim to develop character, compassion and service. Thoughout their time here, pupils are excpected to contribute to our school community and to society. We want children to try things they cannot do, to persist in the face of difficulty and to become resilient in overcoming obstacles. This is 'the William Hulme's Way".

With this in mind, we provide a breadth of opportunities and experiences which seek to help our students become confident, well-rounded and ambitious young adults. Our curriculum and enrichment programme is overflowing with opportunities to try something new and develop new skills.

Top both pages: *School photograph, 2011.* ***Right:*** *Mr Peter Mulholland, Principal.*

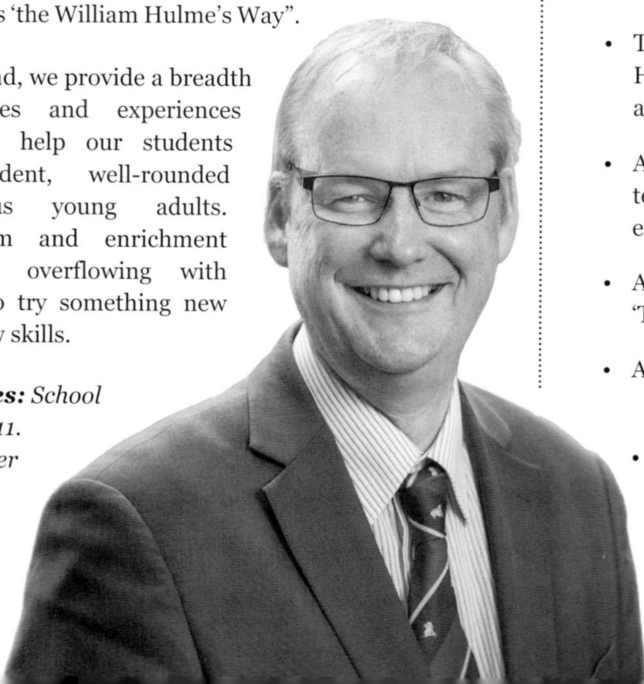

NEW AND DIFFERENT EXPERIENCES

In addition to our very wide range of extracurricular clubs, our students enjoy trips to activity centres, performing in front of their friends and families, university visits, talks from inspirational speakers as well as countless opportunities to collaborate with their peers at United Learning schools across the country.

We are incredibly proud to deliver an 'Education with Character'; an education which challenges, inspires and excites our students and prepares them for the ups and downs of life.

No two days are the same at William Hulme's Grammar School; our children are constantly introduced to new and different experiences, designed to prepare them for the next stage of their education and beyond.

The reason we believe William Hulme's to be one of the most popular and highest performing state schools in the UK is we provide the following to our students:

- An all-through 3 - 18 school experience
- A learning environment based on very high academic standards
- A school where all children are encouraged to reach their true potential and parents are welcome
- The best of the independent school tradition such as the House system and a tremendous range of extracurricular activities
- An exciting place to learn with excellent facilities, new technology and a wide range of teaching and learning experiences
- A vibrant and tolerant multi cultural community 'Trust, but in Whom Take Care'
- A deeper learning of the wider world through our enterprise activities and International School links
- Outstanding careers advice and an opportunity to meet ex-students who have been successful in a variety of occupations.

MULTI-CULTURAL COMMUNITY

William Hulme's is a multi-cultural community and values highly harmony, tolerance and understanding. The school has an international outlook and provides exciting opportunities and links for all its students. William Hulme's is committed to building on the success that it has achieved so far, welcoming involvement from the local community and being part of the United Learning group that is committed to bringing out 'the best in everyone'.

The Manchester Evening News recently reported that it is the most popular primary and secondary school in the whole of Greater Manchester. The school has a higher ratio of first choice applications for a place than any of the Trafford grammar schools.

Success has also attracted the attention of the national press, with the Daily Telegraph featuring the school in its lead article on admissions. 'William Hulme's' strong reputation is rooted in continued academic success. In 2018, the school won two national awards for the progress and attainment of its pupils.

The school is also making good progress at A Level with over 90% of students going on to study at university. Students continue to gain Oxbridge success and all of our students move on to excellent courses or training. Old Hulmeians are encouraged to come into school and share the secrets of their successful careers with the current generation of students.

The school has recently undergone an impressive expansion programme thanks to the support of Manchester Local Authority. It now boasts a brand new state of the art two form entry Primary Phase, enhanced modern facilities throughout the Secondary Phase, including an impressive Music Centre and a beautifully refurbished Sixth Form Centre in the old building that brings together the distinctive tradition and ethos of the school and modern technology that enhances the education of its students.

The school, its staff, governors, pupils and parents have embraced great change and will continue to move forward and make William Hulme's the best school in the Greater Manchester region.

OLYMPIAN BRINGS THE GOLDEN TOUCH TO PRESENTATION EVENING

In 2016, Rio Olympic Gold medalist Alex Danson MBE helped William Hulme's Grammar School honour its own superstars, with a presentation event celebrating the school's exam success.

In the school's Great Hall, Chair of Governors David Marsden and Principal Peter Mulholland welcomed guests to the event, with students across all year groups rewarded for their hard work, which this summer saw 75% of Year 11s gain the new government measure of 9 - 4 grades in both English and maths at GCSE, as well as an increase of 6% in the number of A level entries achieving A to B grades.

Supporting the event in her role as a United Learning Sports Ambassador was Alex, a member of Team GB's Olympic gold medal winning Women's Hockey Squad, who helped present the awards, with prizes in all subject areas, as well as recognition from Heads of Year.

Go Goodwins

Travelling the roads in style!

A Manchester family can proudly boast of having been involved in coach travel since the early part of the 20th century.

Go Goodwins has been transporting people around the city and beyond since 1976 but its roots stem from York Motors which was formed in 1917.

Back then, the travelling customers could only dream of the comfort and style which would be enjoyed by future generations travelling with Go Goodwins.

The first motor coaches came into use in the early 1900s and the first scheduled coach service was launched in 1925 between London and Bristol.

In the 1920s the new coach industry benefited from a big boost as numerous independent companies entered the new and growing market and rules and regulations followed. The Road Traffic Act was passed in 1930 which included for the first time, a speed limit.

The Second World War put the British coach market effectively out of order, as all services had to be suspended in order to save fuel. The coaches run by York Motors became part of the war effort and used for whatever purposes were deemed necessary at that time.

Coach operators had been left wondering what the cancellation of services might mean for the industry once the war was over. But, any fears were soon dismissed as the post-war years were prosperous times for the coach and bus industry. Few people could afford cars and used coach and bus travel for their road journeys.

The late Alan Edward Goodwin and his wife, Carol, are responsible for putting Go Goodwins on the road. He was the grandson of the founder of York Motors and started working with his grandfather as a mechanic at the business which was then working out from Chorlton Cum Hardy. Shortly afterwards Alan and Carol were running their own business from their council house in Benchill, Wythenshaw, with Carol responsible for the administrative tasks.

Above: *Alan Edward Goodwin started working with his Granddad at York Motors as a mechanic.* ***Left:*** *Alan Goodwin, Geoff's grandfather.* ***Below:*** *An old single-decker.*

They were later joined by son Geoff in 1978, and shortly afterwards were operating from a yard in Sharston and the business was expanding and able to purchase its first, new, mini bus. New premises were bought in Stockport in 1980 as more contracts were won and the business was building a reputation working with sports teams which included the Altrincham Aces Ice Hockey team which later became Trafford Metros before reforming and changing back to the original name.

Left: *Geoff's first AEC coach.* **Below:** *Goldliner Volvo B10M Geoff's coach, 1984.*

That reputation of successfully working with sports teams was catapulted further into the limelight in the mid-1980s when the business won a contract to transport Manchester United Football Club when Ron Atkinson was manager.

Above: *Wes & Sally Goodwin.* **Below:** *Some of Go Goodwins old coaches.*

As time progressed so did the quality of coach travel and in 1989 Goodwins bought their first new Volvo Jonckheere high-tech coach which came with bathroom facilities, chill-out area, TV and all the trimmings. Thousands of customers enjoyed luxury travel as it made numerous trips all over Europe.

The 1990s was an eventful decade for Go Goodwins and started with the business opening its own MoT testing station and then moving to larger premises at Salford, after buying out Erics Way Coaches and needing larger premises for the expanded fleet.

Alan and Carol's grandson, Wesley, was the next generation to stop onboard to start his career learning about the business. But, soon, the family business was to face its toughest challenge yet. In 1995 an aggressive blaze on the eve of Bonfire Night wiped out its whole fleet of coaches. The family and their staff were left with a huge uphill struggle but were determined the Goodwins name would survive.

Survive, it did, supported by a strong and loyal client base and industry contacts and by the end of the 1990s it was thriving again winning one of its biggest contracts with the England Cricket Board. With Go Goodwins operating the more stylish and bespoke coaches for higher end use they were sought after and rented out to some of the world's top artists, including Justin Timberlake and Britney Spears.

The England Cricket Board contract was developed and by 2001 the full and official coach contract for the ECB was obtained. In 2010 Goodwins started working with the Greater Manchester Passenger Transport Executive providing bus services around

North and South Mancheser. The business transferred its bus operations to Rotala in 2017 to again concentrate on its coach operations. The sale included 19 buses, a freehold depot and the transfer of bus service contracts which were rebranded Diamond Bus under the Rotala umbrella.

Above: *Fleet in Eccles, 1997.* ***Inset:*** *Go Goodwin's first brand new coach in 1989, now back at the depot undergoing restoration.* ***Below:*** *Three generations of Goodwins in 1989.*

Go Goodwins, headquartered at the Lyntown Trading Estate, Eccles, continues to operate a fleet of 20 plus coaches and buses on corporate, private hire and school contracts which includes its cricket and football contracts.

It took over the coach business of Ashall's of Manchester, also in 2017, which included contracts and three coaches. The coaches include an Irizar PB Scania which has been used by the England football team and the South African cricket team.

Go Goodwins has coaches for hire for all occasions such as day trips, concerts, airport transfers, and weddings. The company also organises its own day trips to popular occasions and holidays which are scheduled throughout the year in an annual brochure. Coach holidays are inclusive of day trips, admissions, boat trips, train rides etc, in addition to the extras customers have come to expect, like morning coffee and biscuits, sweets and snacks served on board using Staffordshire china. Afternoon tea and light lunches are also served on board on some holidays. Hotels used tend to be four star and all have spa facilities/ swimming pools to ensure the style on the coach is continued at destination.

The top-end luxury coaches operated by Go Goodwins can even be configurated so the layout and seating arrangements are suitable for the booking. A Team Class coach is ideal for extended tours and is used by the England and Wales Cricket Board for carrying touring teams as well as the England Cricket Team. The Hospitality Class coaches are an ideal solution for long distance road trips where living on the road is required.

In fact, all solutions are catered for – including those bookings for where a vintage coach is preferred - and the level of high class services and attention to detail should ensure Go Goodwins continues motoring along into the distant future.

As a local company, Go Goodwins are proud of its roots and plays an active role in supporting the community and their business partners. They are the official team sponsor and coach provider to Manchester Storm and has a long history of supporting ice hockey at Altrincham rink. Additionally, Go Goodwins sponsor Altrincham Aces. They are also team sponsors of Accrington Stanley FC, Newton Le Willows Cricket Club, Reddish North End FC and St Andrew's All Stars FC, Lee Fairhurst and Stuart Smith Formula 1 Stock car racers.

Four generations of Goodwins. ***Top:*** *Wesley's 1st new coach in 2001.*

Hadfield Wood Recyclers

The heart of a Manchester family business

Keeping it in the family is the key to success for Manchester's Hadfield Wood Recyclers, which has four generations working in the business almost 40 years after it was originally formed.

GI Hadfield and Son Ltd began life in 1980 as a skip hire business, based at its current site in Droylsden - originally the Hadfield's family farm.

Left: *Geoff Hadfield and Grandad in September 2018.*

After a while MD Geoff Hadfield realised there was a volume of waste wood coming in on the skips which was being sent to landfill. Through research Geoff discovered the panel board industry was looking for feedstock to manufacture its own products and that with the right processing, waste wood could be used for this industry.

He invested £1 million in bespoke cleaning plant to ensure he could process the waste wood into a viable and sustainable wood chip product, and so Hadfield Wood Recyclers was born.

In 1997 Hadfield signed its first wood contract with a panel board producer, CSC Forest Products. Once established as a manufacturer of panel board feedstock, Geoff was keen to find alternative uses for his investment.

As an ex-farmer he knew there was a need for affordable, sustainable and consistently available animal beddings. He began producing bedding for horses and in 1999, following a further £1m of plant upgrades, Hadfield launched its easibed equine bedding product.

Today Hadfield Wood Recyclers is one of the UK's oldest and biggest wood recyclers, processing more than 300,000 tonnes a year of waste wood into recycled and sustainable products.

Geoff is a founder, former Chair and current Board member of the Wood Recyclers' Association – the industry's trade body. Having originally set up the business with his wife Sue, Geoff remains MD of Hadfield Wood Recyclers, with his father "Grandad Geoff", his daughter Cherie, son "young Geoff" and two of his grandchildren now working in the business as well.

The company has a Board of Directors who oversee the growth and development of the business on a day-to-day basis.

Hadfield still supplies panel board feedstock to the UK's biggest manufacturers, but it is also now well-known for its range of award-winning dust-free animal beddings including easibed as well as easichick for poultry and easicattle for dairy cows.

The company operates from three sites, Manchester, Middlesbrough and Tilbury in Essex, offering a truly nationwide service. It handles waste wood for many national and international waste management companies, local authorities and other public sector bodies, as well as businesses from all industries including construction, waste and retail.

One of its proudest achievements has been winning the largest wood contract in the UK in 2001 - which at the time was 7000 tonnes a year - with the former Greater Manchester Waste Disposal Authority (GMWDA). It has since seen this increase to over 40,000 tonnes a year. This contract has been sustained through Hadfield's responsiveness to the ever-changing demands of busy household waste recycling sites including the provision of flexible opening hours during peak periods and ongoing staff training to ensure the best efficiency was achieved for the individual local authorities that made up GMWDA.

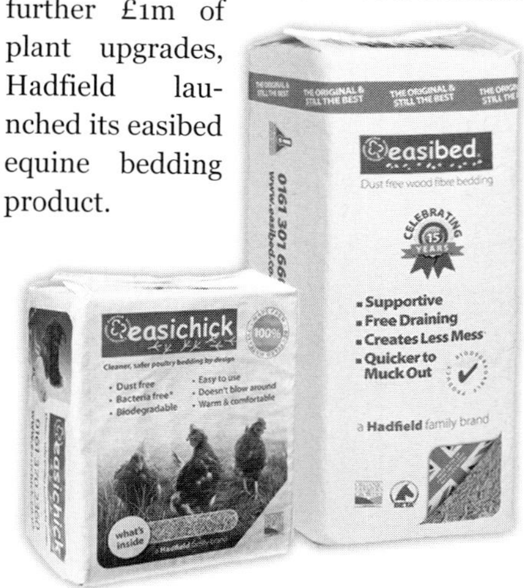

Left: *HWR animal bedding bales easichick and easibed.*

Above: Hadfield Wood Recyclers Manchester site in 2018.
***Inset:** The original farm site.*

Innovation

Hadfield's ability to lead in every marketplace it enters is due to its innovative attitude.

When easibed was launched it was the first alternative horse bedding on the market and took the equestrian world by storm. Almost two decades later it is as popular as ever. It's a dust-free, absorbent and free-draining bedding, especially beneficial for horses with respiratory problems.

Prior to easibed's launch the equine market had never been able to buy a manufactured bedding able to meet particular requirements. easibed also introduced the market to bedding manufactured from a recycled material and invested heavily in educating horse owners as to its safety in the face of fears of contamination. Today a big part of easibed's appeal is that it is a recycled product.

easibed won a UK export award in 2008 and is used by horse riders, trainers and owners around the world including international show jumpers Ellen Whitaker, Michael Whitaker and Billy Twomey as well as many amateur riders rising from grassroots through the ranks.

***Right:** International show jumper Ellen Whitaker uses easibed.*

Hadfield's poultry bedding easichick, another award-winning product, was originally developed for the commercial poultry market and is used by many of the leaders in the UK's poultry industry, including Bernard Matthews, Moy Park and Cranberry Foods.

The wood fibre bedding is treated with a organic additive making it bio-secure and free from bacterias and moulds that cause problems for poultry and other birds. Hadfield was also the first bedding company to develop a unique blower trailer system to ensure the poultry bedding was delivered directly into the sheds to eliminate any cross contamination and the spread of avian flu.

In 2013 Hadfields launched a 10kg branded bale of easichick to the consumer market, for back-yard poultry keepers, small holders and other birds. In total Hadfield produces seven different types of poultry bedding. All have been developed in response to customer demand and feedback.

Following hot-on-the-heels of easichick came dairy bedding easicattle, a reduced dust wood fibre bedding designed specifically for dairy cattle and treated with an organic additive. Tests have shown that over a period of time cows on easicattle remain cleaner and stay healthier, helping reduce their likelihood of infection, making it a popular choice for dairy farmers around the UK.

All of the easi beddings have the coveted Organic Farmers and Growers certification.

Above: *Hadfield produce easicattle for dairy cows.* ***Below:*** *Loader in factory with wood chip.*

Expansion and Investment

In more recent years Hadfield has added wood chip biomass fuel to the 20 plus products it manufactures.

In 2007 it launched a sister company, UK Wood Recycling based at Redcar near Middlesbrough in the north east. UK Wood Recycling supplies high specification biomass fuel to Sembcorp Utilities Ltd for the UK's first wood-derived biomass boiler - Wilton 10 - which generates electricity for the national grid.

***Above:** A Hadfield lorry heading out on a delivery. **Below:** Hadfield Wood Recyclers loading a boat with wood chip biomass fuel.*

In 2008 it secured a contract with Veolia Essex and opened its third site at the Port of Tilbury in Essex, which processes 140,000 tonnes of waste wood a year. The company has a 12-year agreement for exclusive waste wood import and export rights over the quay at the port.

In 2015 the company invested a further £2m to expand to a new site at Tilbury Docks which is now a hub of wood collection from the south of England and has created the ideal base from which to ship the company's panelboard and biomass products to European plants. It has enabled Hadfield to become the UK's biggest exporters of recycled wood into Europe.

In 2016 Hadfield invested a further £3.4m to expand its Droylsden site into one of the largest bespoke recycling facilities in the UK with the addition of six acres.

The following year it completed the expansion of an additional 10 acre site at Middlesbrough with a further £1m of investment, increasing the size of the site to 21 acres.

In 2018 Hadfield agreed a new contract with Sembcorp Utilities Ltd to continue to supply the Wilton 10 biomass power station until March 2027.

Investment in all three of its sites also involved work to ensure they complied with new health & safety and environmental legislation, and to improve service levels. This included installing the UK's first thermal imaging fire prevention technology system to monitor and detect heat changes in wood piles and raise an alarm if heat is detected above acceptable levels. The system will ensure the fastest possible detection if an issue arises.

The result has seen Hadfield win RoSPA Gold Awards for health and safety for three consecutive years.

Social Responsibility

Despite its expansion and growth into a national recycler employing over 160 people, Hadfield has remained a true family business at heart and takes its social responsibility very seriously.

The company has strong links with residents' associations and charities in each of the areas where it has sites and takes pride in supporting community events and local causes.

As Geoff always says to his employees and family: "you are only as good as the people you've got around you". And he knows that employing local people and working with local causes is part of what makes Hadfield the success it is.

J. Allcock & Sons
Recycling rubber around the world

James Allcock began his business, J Allcock & Sons Ltd, in 1924. The company started in Audenshaw, then in 1928 there was a move to Soapery Street, (later to become Textile Street), in West Gorton.

These premises were on the site of a former wood yard and a Chapel. Mr Allcock turned the Sunday School building into a warehouse for his business which provided chemicals to the emerging rubber industry in the Manchester area. The business was incorporated in May 1928.

The Second World War was a profitable time for Allcocks. The availability of natural rubber was much reduced, so demand for factice (a rubber substitute) was high and profitable. The high demand for proofed fabric meant that Allcocks could sell all that they could manufacture.

The founder's two sons continued the business, but the third generation had other interests. One of the founder's grandchildren, for instance, is James Allcock, the Radio Vet who also wrote magazine articles about animals. The family business was sold to the Anchor Chemical Company in Clayton. Before starting his own business James Allcock had worked for Anchor making factice.

As well as the production of factice, Allcocks started to sell other products required in the rubber industry.

Anchor ran its new purchase as one of its subsidiaries and used its facilities to make various factices. These rubber substitutes are used in the manufacture of soft rubber compounds such as erasers, proofed fabrics and hoses.

This process was continued and extended by Anchor who used Allcocks as a trading house for distributed products that would appear to present a conflict of interests with distribution agreements they had.

Mr R. S. Rushton, who eventually became chairman, worked his way up in the company from a post in the laboratory at Anchor Chemical, through the position of Works Director. He became responsible for the running of Allcocks and decided to buy out the company and run it with his wife Margaret.

At the time the Rushton family took over, the firm consisted of a very small three-office building, the original warehouse, a second warehouse, a works and a portacabin used as a canteen. Mr Rushton ran the concern with three other staff and one part-timer.

Five years later, Allcocks acquired Truscott (or Diamond) Transport Company and its property next door.. Allcocks also had its eye on an area of waste land at the rear of their site and bordered by Ambrose Street, which in the past had been a Starch Works, then the Openshaw Brewery and then a paper mill. In 1982, an old chain factory became available, which was bought and a Rubber Recycling plant was installed to manufacture granules for sports and play surfaces, and rubber dust (we call crumb) that gets used back in all rubber compounds.

Top: *J Allcock Snr., extreme left, and J Allcock Jnr., third left.* ***Above:*** *J Allcock Jnr., front with his motorbike.* ***Left:*** *James Allcock Junior who founded the business along with his father James Allcock Senior.*

Unfortunately the Ambrose Street Works was destroyed by fire in May 1992 as the result of arson. Those responsible were never found. The fire started on the roof over the workshop. The pitch on the roof melted through and dropped into the storage area on to 110 metric tonnes of rubber crumb (dust) and granules. The resultant fire devastated the building. The insurers even wrote off the foundations. As well as the building and its contents, it demolished three fork lift trucks and a travelling overhead crane. Though damaged by smoke and water, the offices survived.

It took three-and-a-half years to settle the insurance claim before plans for the future could be made. The Works were rebuilt, on the Ambrose Street site. Meanwhile business had continued in rented premises in Mossley and thus a minimum customer base was retained.

At the same time sterling fell out of the ERM and, as the majority of distributed products were imported, prices went up by 20% overnight. The company survived all this and emerged stronger and more focused.

***Above:** The factice manufacturing team in 1973, from left, Jim Holmes, Joe Cuttle and Ted McCarley.* ***Below:** Ronald Rushton signing a distribution agreement with the world's largest silicone company, Dow-Corning in 1973.*

Today, the company is still deeply involved with the rubber industry but it also distributes compounding chemicals into plastics and surface coatings. We also grind and granulate cured rubber scrap so that can be recycled, using what we consider one of the most modern grinding facilities in the UK.

The company provides problem-free deliveries of the correct material on the right day, with the right paperwork and at an economical price. Mr and Mrs Rushton retired from the day-to-day running of the company in 1989, although Mr Rushton remained as the company's chairman. Mr Bob Howard ran the company until his retirement at the end of 1996. Bob Howard was replaced by Andrew Rushton as Managing Director with his brother David as Works Director.

Above left: Mr Bob Howard who retired in 1996. ***Left:** One of Allcocks wagons with a pallet of reclaimed rubber imported from Czechoslovakia.*

Above: *Land acquired in 1980 for the expansion of the company.* ***Right:*** *The fire which destroyed part of the factory on the 16th May 1992.*

In 1997 the company's commitment to quality was reinforced with the attainment of the first Quality Standard of BS5750. This has been kept and improved ever since and in 2016 the company achieved ISO 9001-2015 and are the first and only Rubber Recycling Company to achieve this standard.

In 1999 Allcocks made its first acquisition when they were approached by Mr. David Birkett who owned the Wellington Rubber Co. Ltd in Leeds and was the son of the founder. He was of an age when he wanted to take a step back and start planning for a much deserved retirement. He thought Allcocks ethos fitted in very well with his own and suggested Allcocks might be interested in acquiring the business. Wellington Rubber Co. was a 100% rubber recycling unit, able to sell everything they managed to produce and so understandably, this was of great interest to Allcocks.

Wellington's main business is buying buffings from Truck Tyre Retreaders. Every Truck Tyre gets retreaded a number of times in its life. They buff off the old tread and what comes off is called buffings. They buy over 3,000 metric tonnes per year that they process into different sizes. In the ensuing months, Wellington Rubber Co. was incorporated into Allcocks and relocated within the Manchester site in 2002, allowing David Birkett to gradually let go of the reigns until in 2005, he retired. Wellington Rubber is now run by Adrian France who used to work for a similar company who were a competitor, a supplier, a customer and a friend all in one. Wellington Rubber Co. has become so successful that they have had to move that business to a bigger site at Wimpory Street and they are looking to expand further.

From 1999 onwards our main aim has been to strengthen our position in the recycling of rubber. The old rubber industry in this country was changing and the lower quality, lower price work was moving abroad. So we

Left: *The new crumb plant.* ***Above:*** *Mr. Andrew Rushton (left) and* Mr. David Birkett (right).

comes from our export business.

The majority of export business comes from custom grinding of our customers own scrap. We call this our "Laundry Business". Customers segregate and deliver the rubber they want recycled. We grind it to the agreed size and then sell them back the reprocessed rubber. They then add this back into their products.

had to adapt our position. We became suppliers of higher value niche products and started to investigate ways to recycle the new lower volume higher value rubbers that were starting to be used.

DEVULCANISATION - In 2006, RAPRA (Rubber and Plastic Research Association) invited Allcocks and a number of other like minded rubber people to join a consortium to investigate the Devulcanisation of rubber. This has been something scientists have been striving for years to achieve. As we already had some knowledge of the chemistry required and the small success we had achieved to date, we joined forces. The first collaboration was so successful we agreed a second consortium with the name REMOULD. This also was so successful that Allcocks along with two other rubber companies bought the equipment and installed it in Manchester. We now can take customer's own scrap and turn it back into a useful raw material that can go back into the products they make without lowering the quality but at a lower price.

Allcocks and Wellington Rubber Co. now import from Brazil, Czech Republic, Germany, India, Italy, The Netherlands, Sweden, and export all over the world. In fact now 40% of our turnover

Andrew Rushton now has been joined by Keith Devine, who, with his engineering background, is now Operations Director over both Allcocks and Wellington Rubber Co. Government / EU legislation on WASTE put both Companies in a strong position, already having the recycling framework in place; as demand for our services has grown relocating Wellington Rubber Co. has allowed us to increase capacity and efficiency.

Andrew's ability and willingness to react and even anticipate difficult times approaching, was shown in 2017 when the Silicone business was upended globally resulting in shortages and long lead times. By a commitment to stock we have a large increase in the number of silicone customers. Andrew has continued to achieve strong and stable growth – riding the storm of recessions when many around him failed and each time, coming out the other end stronger. His willingness to look further afield to maintain business, both for supplies and sales, has reaped rewards.

Top left: *Mr Rushton, the Chairman of the company pictured with his wife Margaret.* ***Above:*** *Mr Andrew Rushton, the current Managing Director.* ***Below:*** *An aerial view of the premises as they are today.*

M&I Materials Ltd

Commercialising Materials for Demanding Applications

M&I Materials, known world-wide for their innovative products, flexibility, the high quality of their technical knowledge and award-winning customer service, is the parent company behind global market leading brands including Apiezon, Metrosil, MIDEL and Wolfmet.

From their base in Trafford Park, they work in partnership with leading universities and research facilities around the world to commercialise materials for cutting-edge industries, from power and aerospace, to nuclear medicine and high-performance motorsports. The company now exports to over 60 countries from their Manchester base and with international offices and production facilities expanding across the Americas, Africa, Middle East, Europe and Asia Pacific, the company has the local knowledge, language skills and the agility to respond rapidly to their customers needs.

The Apiezon range of high vacuum greases, sealants and lubricant waxes are trusted around the world for their quality, consistency and excellent performance in vacuum applications.

For more than 80 years, Metrosil, the innovative range of non-linear resistors, has been trusted globally to provide high energy, high voltage electrical surge protection.

MIDEL is the world's leading range of biodegradable ester-based dielectric fluids for transformers, chosen by customers who want to reduce the risk

Above: *The Micanite and Insulators Co. Limited Stansted factory.*

of fire, prevent environmental damage and significantly extend transformer life.

Wolfmet is a range of world leading tungsten products used for a variety of solutions, from adding weight and balance in aerospace and motorsport applications, to protecting against the effects of X-ray and gamma radiation.

Born out of the research division of GEC Alsthom, M&I Materials Ltd, can trace its roots back to 1901, when twin brothers Arthur and Edward Berkeley laid the foundations when they formed the Mica Insulator Company Ltd to manage the distribution of mica products in Europe. Micanite (the name given to the sheet metal derived from mica) was already readily available in the U.S. and Arthur had seen its potential at Chicago's World Fair.

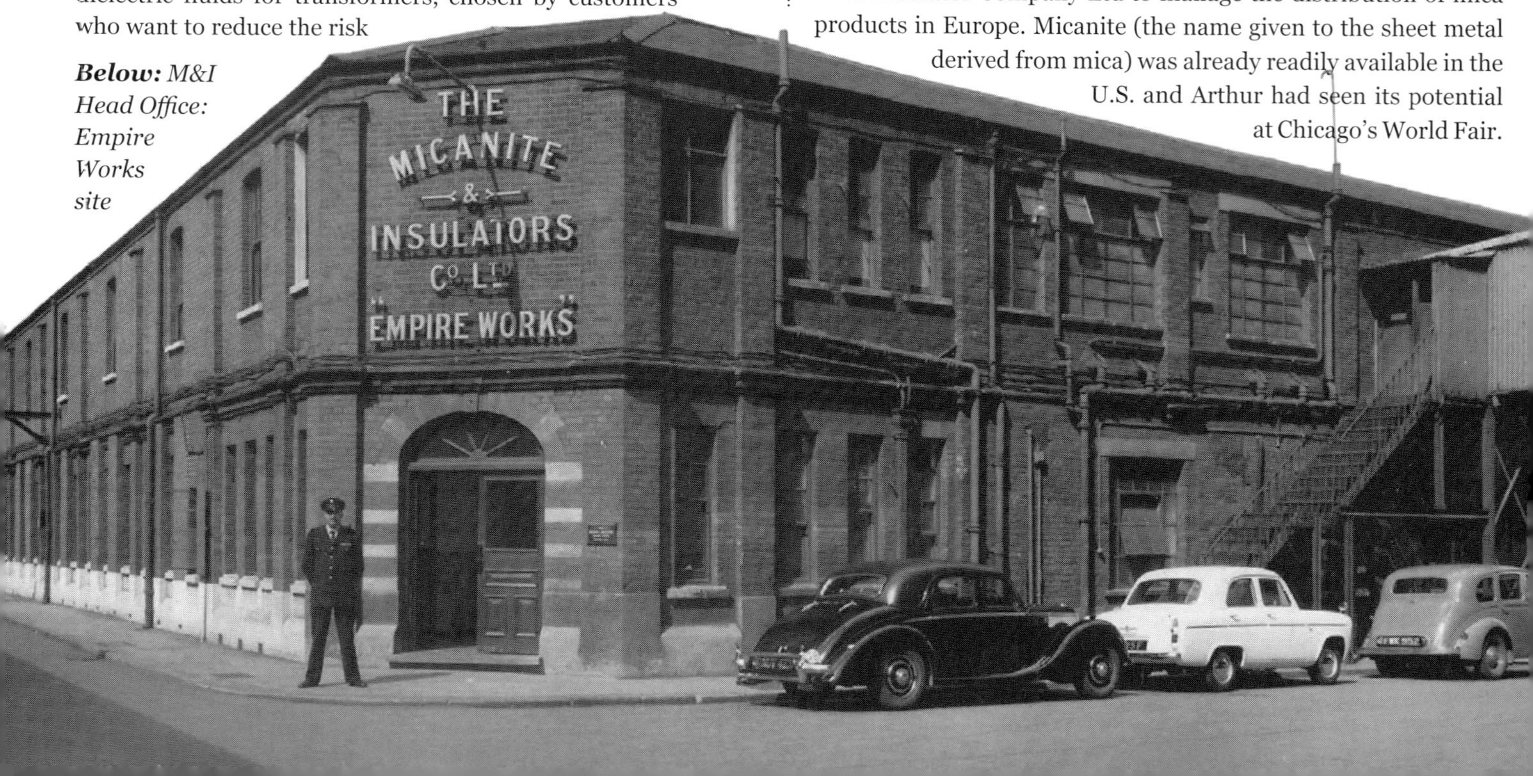

Below: *M&I Head Office: Empire Works site*

The brothers bought a small manufacturing unit in Stoke Newington, London, however growing demand forced a move to Stansted, Essex, before settling at the Empire Works, Walthamstow, London.

In 1906, the firm became known as The Micanite & Insulators Co. Ltd, then later more frequently referred to as simply 'M&I'.

At the time, Micanite had to be painstakingly constructed by hand by brushing shellac varnish over mica splittings that had been laid out. This created a mica sheet that was then dried and pressed before being trimmed and cut to size. Electrical insulation products such as Micanite tubes could be produced in this way. Engineers soon recognised the uses of mica insulation in switchgear. Notable customers included British Thomson-Houston, the General Electric Company and Metropolitan-Vickers, a company that would contribute much to the M&I Materials story.

Throughout its first two decades of trading, the company established itself as a key player in the electrical insulation market through its Micanite manufacture, as well as the production of insulating cloths, tapes, and high-voltage bushings for pylons.

Another important newcomer during this era was the British Westinghouse Electrical & Manufacturing Company, which was founded in 1899 by US industrialist George Westinghouse and renamed the 'Metropolitan Vickers Electrical Company' in 1919 following a takeover by Vickers Ltd. Based in a large heavy engineering facility at Trafford Park, Manchester, 'Metrovicks' became a household name during the first half of the twentieth century and the company's manifold achievements could fill several volumes. The transformers it supplied would pave the way for the installation of the National Grid and most significantly for M&I Materials, its research department would produce a wealth of engineering innovations, some of which are still in production today.

Low-vapour pressure oils were developed by Metrovicks in the mid-1920s and named Apiezon. Soon, Apiezon pumps became a groundbreaking product. Meanwhile, in 1929, Associated Electrical Industries (AEI) was created, amalgamating Metrovicks with its rival, British Thomson Houston and other electrical companies.

Above: *Products manufactured during the late-1930s, including punchings, end rings, Empire tapes and Paxolin laminates.* ***Left:*** *Bill Burch at work in the Metrovicks research department.*

Apiezon oil was also incorporated into a paste and wax that opened up new opportunities for its use.

The high-voltage department of Metrovicks Research was also making progress in the field of electrical insulation and Metrosil was developed at the Trafford Park site. Metrosil marked a significant departure from the existing understanding of resistant materials. In fact, it is widely believed that Metrosil was the first resistor to work as a Voltage Surge Diverter.

Metrosil production had begun in 1937 and preparations for war had already commenced at Metrovicks. Searchlights, automatic pilot systems, radar and gun mountings had all entered into production under government contracts.

Right: *The impressive high-voltage laboratory.*

However, the increased government interest in Metrovicks also brought unwelcome attention from Germany. Just one month after war had been declared, the Trafford Park works were photographed by the Luftwaffe and individual buildings were identified with remarkable accuracy. The first bombs fell on the factory on the 22nd December 1940, causing severe damage to the works area. Despite this severe setback and rumours abounding that the works were 'done for', the roofless machine shops were soon covered and production reached 80% of normal levels just four weeks after the bombings had taken place. A royal visit from the King and Queen in February 1941 brought a further boost to morale.

In Walthamstow, the Micanite and Insulator Company was also diversifying as a result of the necessities of war. The company's Paxolin brand found new applications as a durable and weight-for-weight stronger alternative to aluminium that could be used in aircraft instrument panels, aerial masts and special types of bomb cases.

In the short-term, both the Micanite and Insulator Company and Metrovicks research enjoyed a boom in the post-war period, although changes were afoot for both companies.

While Metrovicks reconverted to non-military production, there was much discussion about the direction that future research activities should take. In Walthamstow, additional demand for electrical insulation stimulated the business and the Micanite and Insulator Company enjoyed the privilege of being the sole provider of mica paper to the UK market. At the time the Micanite and Insulator Company had a superb reputation within the electrical industry, and officially joined the Associated Electrical Industries (AEI) group in 1958, having already produced components for the group's subsidiaries since the late 1920s.

Research departments at Metrovicks and British Thompson-Houston were combined into the AEI Research Laboratory which expanded its scope with advances in radar and broadcasting.

Above: *Wolfmet furnace in operation.* ***Left:*** *1981 advert praising MIDEL as an environmentally friendly alternative to PCBs.*

In 1967, AEI (and with it, M&I, the AEI Research Laboratory and several other firms) was acquired by the General Electric Company (GEC) for an agreed fee of £120 million, with the industrialist Arnold Weinstock assuming control of the group and all its subsidiaries.

The new owners took the decision to close Micanite and Insulator's Walthamstow plant and move its production to the Trafford Park site. During GEC's restructuring programme, Trafford Park became a repository for a variety of industrial activities such as die-casting, the AEI Research Laboratory and copper alloys, Metrosil and Apiezon production. For many working within the AEI Research Laboratory, their work altered dramatically.

The department had always been a consumer of products, investigating new applications and developing new innovations, whereas it was now a manufacturing department, combined with the production that had been moved up from Walthamstow.

The next innovation was the development of MIDEL transformer fluid. Researchers had spotted a gap in the market for a transformer fluid that, unlike existing PCB-based products, combined the necessary properties with an environmentally friendly formation. MIDEL was patented in 1979. MIDEL was first used in transformers built by GEC Broadstairs for the British Steel factory at Port Talbot. It was later developed for use on railways which today still remains an important market for MIDEL around the world.

The 1980s brought a move into the production of heavy alloys, triggered by GEC's acquisition of Elmet Alloys Ltd, of Warrington,

Left: *Heavy alloys produced by M&I Materials.*

which was moved into Trafford Park. Further acquisitions into the 1990s resulted in M&I becoming a player in the heavy alloy market.

Left: *Colin Salt and Steve Jeffery attend a reception for 2009 Queen's Award winners, hosted by Her Majesty The Queen.*

Notable progress was made in the field of tungsten heavy alloys when M&I commenced production of tungsten heavy alloys in 1989, which for the Elmet brand, marked a shift from producing alloys en-masse to producing specific components. As M&I looked to market its new product abroad, an alternative product name was needed as an American firm was already registered under the Elmet name. 'Wolfram' is the Latin word for tungsten and is a more recognisable term for the metal in many European languages.

Since its inception, Wolfmet has demonstrated its suitability for a staggering array of applications, from aerospace to nuclear to high performance motorsport.

Also, in 1989, there was a merger between the power generation and transport arm of GEC and the French company Compagnie General D'Electricite (GCE) after which M&I became known as GEC ALSTHOM (M&I Ltd). The conglomerate began to move into large scale manufacturing activity rather than components and in 1993 there was a management buyout of M&I by the then Managing Director, Colin Salt. It was agreed that the newly named M&I Materials Ltd, would acquire the Apiezon, Metrosil, MIDEL and Wolfmet products.

Above: *M&I Materials opens USA office in Atlanta, Georgia to support MIDEL's expansion.* **Right:** *Apiezon is trusted globally for its quality, consistency and excellent performance in vacuum applications.* **Below:** *Head Office, Hibernia Way.*

A significant period of modernisation and investment followed which grew the company at home and abroad, and in June 2003, the firm moved premises to the current purpose-built site at Hibernia Way, Trafford Park.

As M&I was the last original building standing on the Trafford Park site, the move spelled the official demise of GEC's old premises and turned a decisive page in Manchester's industrial history.

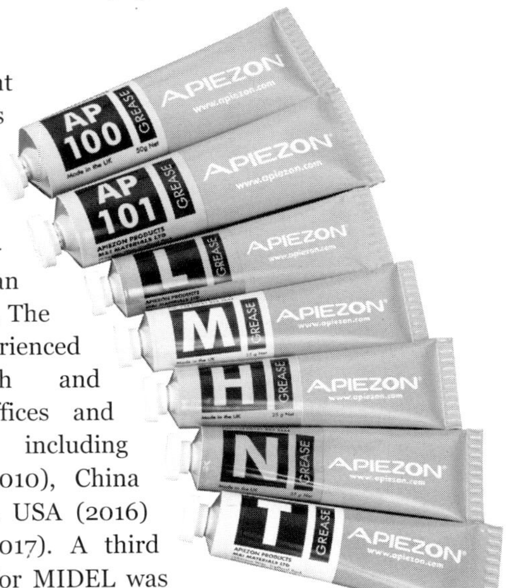

Throughout this current decade, with Giles Salt as CEO, M&I Materials has continued to enjoy the flexibility that comes with being an independent company. The company has experienced considerable growth and invested in new offices and production facilities including opening in India (2010), China (2011), Dubai (2016), USA (2016) and South Africa (2017). A third new production line for MIDEL was added to the Manchester factory in 2018 and with further development of its four leading brands, is now a global market leader in: Fire safe, biodegradable, ester-based dielectric fluids; end-to-end production of tungsten alloy; surge protection solutions to safeguard electrical power networks and high vacuum greases, sealants and lubricants.

M&I Materials owes its success to the countless men and women, past and present, who have built the company into what it is today. The present generation maintains these high standards, by opening doors to new markets and continuing to develop truly innovative, global products. The M&I Materials story is one of a unique fusion of tradition and progress, which strives to commercialise materials for the most demanding of applications, whilst continuing in the spirit of its rich heritage.

Temperature Control

Reducing energy without compromising comfort

Huge strides continue to be made in the air conditioning market and Manchester company Temperature Control, with a long and proud history, is at the forefront of this growing industry. They have built a business on traditional values, while maintaining an open mind to new technologies. The business has expanded into four offices across the UK giving it a countrywide footprint and it has grown into one of the specialist comfort cooling and heating contractors in the country.

It all began in 1899 when E. O. Walker & Co Ltd was founded to support the new electricity technology, which was being widely introduced. Initially, he provided moving pictures on a projector screen which he carried round to large houses of the well-to-do and to any other buildings that had electricity at that time. Mr Walker could have proudly claimed he was among the first to grasp the commercial opportunities of the new silent movie industry.

Electricity was the wonder of the age at the turn of the 20th century and although we have come to take it for granted today not so many generations ago it was very much a novelty. Although, electricity had been around for a while it was still not much of practical use to the ordinary man on the street. Electricity seeped into most people's lives only be degrees. First by the electric telegraph followed by the telephone.

Mass familiarity with electricity came with the electric trams. There were no household appliances with need for electricity until the electric light bulb was invented by Swann and Edison towards the end of the 19th century and then everybody longed to switch from gas mantles to the far superior electric lighting.

Whilst new technologies have been developed over the decades the core values followed by E. O. Walker & Co, in the early days of strong customer value, safe working practices and installations that are built to last, remain as valuable today within Temperature Control.

E. O. Walker & Co opened a specialist electrical shop in Cannon Street, Manchester, in 1926, to serve the growing trend in electric lighting which included specialist theatre lighting and support for the growing film industry.

By the 1930s the business had expanded into all types of electrical services, including the growing trend in refrigeration with a franchise for the American Kelvinator refrigerator brand, and by this time the foundations of the present company were taking shape.

Top left: *Company founder, Mr E O Walker.* ***Above right:*** *Mr H P Walker who took over the running of the firm in 1942.* ***Above:*** *An early delivery vehicle.* ***Right:*** *The interior of the first premises.*

The founder was followed in the business by his son HP Walker who took over from him in 1942. The company maintained the Cannon St store and the electrical goods offered increased over this period into all types of domestic white goods. This coincided with the boom years after the Second World War. Even the Queen enjoyed a visit to one of the exhibitions the company held offering the best British and American home appliances.

The firm was sold in the early 1960s to Mr W Latta who continued to run the business as a refrigeration firm under the name of EO Walker Refrigeration Ltd and began to specialise in supplying shops with refrigeration units. Commercial refrigerated display unit were just beginning to become popular at this time. Though refrigerated storage in warehouses had been commonplace for years this was something which was just starting to make its way into shops more widely.

Frozen food was coming to be more widely available and names like Birdseye and Findus were becoming household names for their frozen food which was not only kept in home freezers but was now sold even in corner shops. And not just corner shops, in the early 1960s supermarkets were just beginning their rise to market dominance. Large fridges were common enough in butchers' shops and fish mongers but until now goods had been kept cool for display by putting them out on marble slabs with a generous dollop of crushed ice. Now with ever improving fridge technology, allied with improved materials, such as plastics, whole displays could be refrigerated.

Before buying out EO Walker Mr Latta had been managing Director of Simons Foods in Newton-le-Willows. After buying the business the firm moved to Walker House in Chorlton Street, Old Trafford, and also moved into air conditioning.

During the 1970s the business grew and prospered in a new direction as the company's activities in supplying refrigerated display units slowed. Mr Jeff Mellor had joined the company during this period and later became managing director. He kick-started the next stages of growth into process cooling, cold rooms and the relatively new market for the installation of air conditioning.

Specialist engineers were recruited to assist the continued growth into the 1980s including Steve Grundy who became deputy managing director. The dynamic partnership of the two men led to the air conditioning market becoming the mainstay of the business in the early 1980s which was reflected in the name change to Temperature Control Ltd.

In 1983 the company name was changed from EO Walker Refrigeration to Temperature Control Ltd to reflect the change of focus into air conditioning. In the early years air conditioning had been hard to get off the ground. Fortunately the company had joined the air conditioning market very early on and was poised and ready when it did eventually take off.

With a team of specialists supporting the management, the 1990s saw Temperature Control grow into one of the leading specialist installers in the UK. The company was an early adopter of what was the new VRV(F) air conditioning technology which helped cement the company's reputation for quality and service which included technical back-up which at the time was highly specialised and suited Temperature Control's engineering expertise.

Expansion continued into this century with Jeff and Steve having taken overall control of the company. A key area of growth was within in the hotel industry providing comfort cooling to more than 1,000 bedrooms a year while working closely with air conditioning manufacturers. Other areas of growth included specialist IT/Data cooling, commercial office comfort cooling and the service and maintenance department.

Top: *Mr W Latta who bought the firm in the early 1960s.* ***Above:*** *The first 'custom' built industrial system.* ***Left:*** *The Queen visiting Walker's stand at an exhibition.*

Today, Temperature Control is recognised for setting standards in the industry through its expertise and close working with manufacturers and key clients. This has resulted in the company being involved in bespoke projects such as the trials of R22 replacement refrigerants, introducing CO_2 heat pumps to the UK market, and installing comfort cooling into a 450 bedroomed hotel.

After the retirement of Jeff and Steve in 2016, Wayne Buckley took over as owner and managing director to steer the business through its next stages of development.

It will continue to work closely with air conditioning manufacturers across the world recognising its key to success is the constant focus on quality, combining development and innovation alongside the traditional values and customer service.

Staff are trained in installing equipment from the major air conditioning suppliers and are approved installers by the manufacturers. However, the company has no particular allegiance to any one manufacturer and can therefore select the product most suitable for any particular site.

Air conditioning units sold provide efficient performance and reduced running costs in the colder months with the added bonus of cooling in the summer.

Top: *Tom White with one of the firm's new vans in the 1970s.* ***Above:*** *In 2016, Wayne Buckley took over as owner and Managing Director.* ***Left:*** *Jeff Mellor & Steve Grundy retired in 2016.* ***Below:*** *A Large Commercial Air Conditioning Installation.*

Don't just take our word for it, here's what our clients think:

"...their engineers continually demonstrate their concern for safe practice, attainment of the highest finish and, importantly, show a real sense of team spirit."

"The installation team and supervisor were a pleasure to work with and went 'over and above' to get this job completed to such a high standard."

"It's rare to find a contractor or supplier who understands the relationship with hotel work and achieving our goals."

"Temperature Control supported the developer from initial build right through to tenant occupation..."

Left and below: *A Hybrid VRF System installed at Mitsubishi Headquarters.*

Through building up clients' trust over many years the company works with some of the largest companies in the UK across a range of sectors including the telecoms, hotel, banking and construction industries. This has included Temperature Control installing air conditioning in all the malls and some of the larger stores in the Trafford Centre, the Mal Maison Hotel, Manchester, and the cooling system on top of Blackpool Tower.

The company's vision is to reduce the energy use in the built environment without compromising comfort and service. It values its role of contractor and won't work with any new suppliers until they have been checked to make sure they meet the standards set by Temperature Control.

It believes a high level of quality is the cornerstone to a long-lasting installation and the key to maintaining energy efficiency. Through training and the use of the latest tools and techniques the best possible results are delivered time and time again.

The company is also committed to be on hand at all stages of the life of a piece of equipment which means it doesn't stop working with clients at the installation stage and relationships last the lifetime of the equipment. This commitment ensures the reputation of Temperature Control and that of its clients are maintained.

Below: *Dale Carnegie Training, July 2018.* ***Right:*** *Central plant room at a large office in Manchester.*

The company's fully qualified design teams offer full design services when required as part of design and build projects which has led to installations carried out throughout the UK and Eire, and plant built for export to countries including Holland, Switzerland, Italy, Indonesia, Mexico, and Canada.

Today, the company strives to deliver the best value in terms of comfort, energy use and satisfaction, with an aim to reduce the energy use in the built environment without compromising comfort and service.

Waters Corporation

'Celebrating the past with an eye on the future'

When John Dalton published his atomic theory "New System of Chemical Philosophy" in 1808 it led to ground-breaking developments and his home city region of Manchester becoming a world science centre.

Dalton, a Manchester Quaker and schoolmaster, was also a self-educated chemist, and his theory was derived from, and rested upon, the observation that elements combine in fixed proportions according to their weights.

What became known as Mass Spectrometry is a means of analysing the tiniest amounts of substances to see what they are made up of at the molecular level.

The pioneering work of John Dalton resulted in John Dalton Street in Manchester being named after him. Another Mancunian, Sir Joseph John Thomson, became famous for pushing the scientific boundaries further. He was born at Cheetham Hill and educated at Owens College before going to Cambridge in 1876. He subsequently, became director of the famous Cavendish Laboratory in 1884. He showed part of Dalton's picture of atoms to be not quite true. Thomson claimed the honour of being the person who discovered the electron, the first known subatomic particle.

In 1904, Thomson built an apparatus which allowed streams of electrically charged atoms and similarly charged molecules (collectively known as ions) to be separated according to their mass. This was in effect the very first mass spectrometer, and in 1912 would famously lead to the discovery of the existence of isotopes – slightly different versions of atoms of the same element.

The mass spectrograph subsequently developed by one of Thomson's students in the 1920s, Nobel Prize-winner Francis Aston, allowed the mass, or weight, of atoms and molecules to be measured.

Thomson himself received the 1906 Nobel Prize for Physics and a knighthood in 1908. On his death in 1940, on the eve of the Battle of Britain, such was Thomson's fame that he would be buried in Westminster Abbey near the remains of Isaac Newton. By the time of World War II all the isotopes of naturally occurring elements had been discovered and measured using mass spectrometry.

During the war, the Research Department of the Metropolitan Vickers (MV) Electrical Company at Manchester's Trafford Park, a company already experienced in vacuum engineering, built mass spectrometers for the United Kingdom Department of Scientific and Industrial Research as part of the development of the first atomic weapons. Following the end of the Second World War the Research Department at MV continued to manufacture mass spectrometers for use in the analysis and identification of organic and inorganic substances. The earliest instruments made went to universities and petroleum companies.

The team at the MV Research Department worked, under Robert Craig, on the design and development of high-resolution mass spectrometers. In 1960 Metropolitan Vickers merged with other companies to form Associated Electrical Industries (AEI) and during the next decade became a world leader in the supply of high-resolution mass spectrometers.

In 1968, Robert Craig, foreseeing an unsettled future at AEI following a takeover by GEC, moved to Vacuum Generators (VG) in East Grinstead. VG had been formed in 1962 by Bernard Eastwell and colleagues to manufacture vacuum components. An embryonic mass spectrometer manufacturing programme was launched by Craig, and

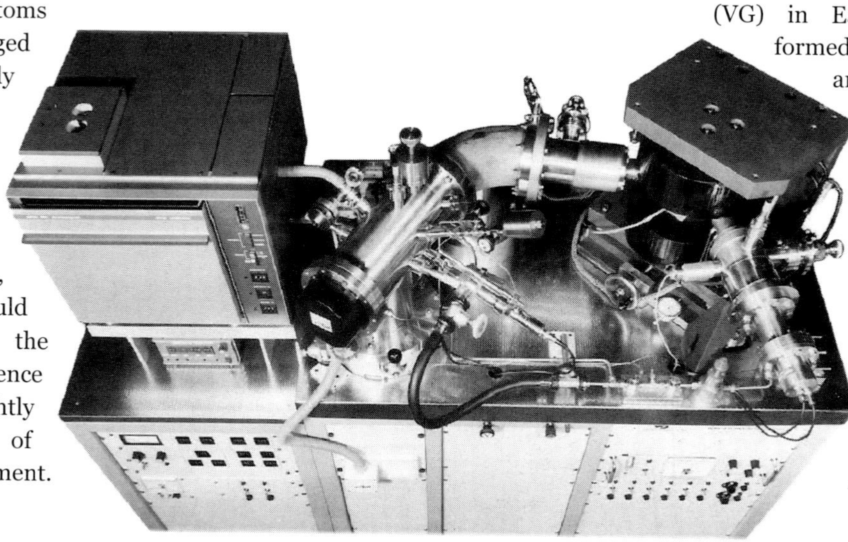

Top left: *Robert Craig, founder of VG Micromass in 1968.* ***Left:*** *A view of the Micromass 70-70 high resolution mass spectrometer, the first new product developed in Altrincham in 1975.*

acquired in 1996 by a management team led by Norman Lynaugh to become the newly constituted Micromass (UK) Ltd.

At the outset Micromass employed some 250 people at its two sites: Broadheath, Altrincham, and Floats Road, Wythenshawe. By 2001, the number of employees in Manchester had swollen to 350 and Micromass opened a third site at Atlas Park, Simonsway, Wythenshawe.

***Above:** An aerial view of Floats Road, Wythenshawe, factory opened in 1981.*

the early instruments were sufficiently successful to encourage the formation of VG Micromass Ltd, which in 1969 with a total of seven staff, moved to Winsford, in Cheshire.

In the 1970s, VG Micromass was split into several new companies, and two of them, VG Organic and VG Data Systems, moved to Broadheath, Altrincham.

VG Organic developed its first high-resolution mass spectrometer, the Micromass 70-70, in 1974. The first instrument was delivered to Oxford University in 1975 and was in use until 1997 when it was decommissioned and presented to the Manchester Museum of Science and Industry.

During the 1980s, VG Organic and VG Data systems were further split up to become VG Analytical, VG Masslab, VG Tritech and VG Biotech – each company selling different types of mass spectrometer to different, but commonly overlapping, markets.

In 1991, the VG Group of Companies, by now owned by British American Tobacco was sold to Fisons plc. Four years later in 1995 Fisons, the then troubled pharmaceutical company, decided to divest itself of its scientific instrument businesses. As a consequence the Manchester-based mass spectrometry companies (VG Analytical, VG BioTech and VG IsoTech) were acquired in 1996 by a management team led by Norman Lynaugh to become the newly constituted Micromass (UK) Ltd.

In 1997, the Waters Corporation, a US-based company with headquarters in Milford near Boston, Massachusetts, acquired Micromass.

In 2000, Micromass won two Queen's Awards, one for International Trade and one for Innovation. These awards were a consequence of the development of the Q-TOF mass spectrometer, a novel tandem quadrupole 'time-of-flight' mass spectrometer that allows detection and identification of less than a pico-gram of a substance. A pico-gram is a millionth of a millionth of a gram, not only too small to be seen with the naked eye but almost too small even to imagine.

By June 2002 Micromass had been fully integrated into Waters and in 2006, Waters introduced a new instrument that not only allows the mass of molecules to be measured but also their shape and size. This instrument, developed in Manchester, is the world's first commercial mass spectrometer to provide this capability.

Two hundred years on since John Dalton developed his atomic theory science and Manchester still remain inextricably linked.

This was cemented further in September 2014, when the Waters Corporation opened its new Mass Spectrometry headquarters in Wilmslow – the world's largest facility committed to the support and development of spectrometers and mass spectrometry systems. The facility, was opened by the then Chancellor George Osborne (above).

***Left:** A group of instruments in development at Floats Road, Wythenshawe, in 1985. The picture shows ZAB-4F - a tandem magnetic sector mass spectrometer and at the time the world's largest commercial mass spectrometer.*

Right: Brian Green, Martin Elliott, Tom Merren and Bob Bateman all worked at AEI in Trafford Park early in their careers so it seemed highly appropriate for them to see the last Autospec leave the Wilmslow facility in December 2015. ***Below:*** *AUTOSPEC-T Tandem Mass Spectrometer 1999. Commercial magnetic sector instruments have a long history in the UK, tracing their origins back to the 1940s and the very early days of mass spectrometry at AEI.*

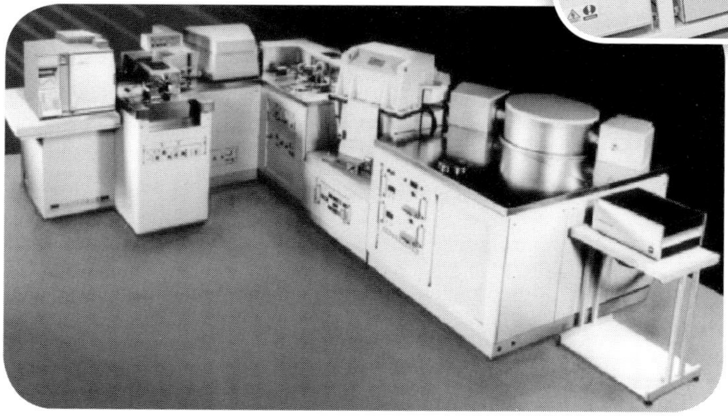

Mr Osborne said: "I am delighted to open the new Waters Corporation offices in Wilmslow, after I helped perform the ground-breaking back in June 2012. It is a fantastic site that provides many excellent local jobs and I wish them every success here in the future."

Brian Smith, Vice President of Mass Spectrometry Operations at Waters, said: "Our new Waters Mass Spectrometry headquarters in Wilmslow marks our continued investment in the region and dedication to the north west. "The new facility has been specially designed to enhance collaboration and drive innovation, building on the research and scores of patents that we have already accomplished in the field, right at the heart of where mass spectrometry first began, here in Manchester."

The new headquarters, which took less than two years to construct from ground-breaking to completion, brings together Waters' existing mass spectrometry centres in the region. The 2,313m^2 building includes state-of-the-art customer demonstration laboratories, research and development capabilities and an expanded manufacturing capacity.

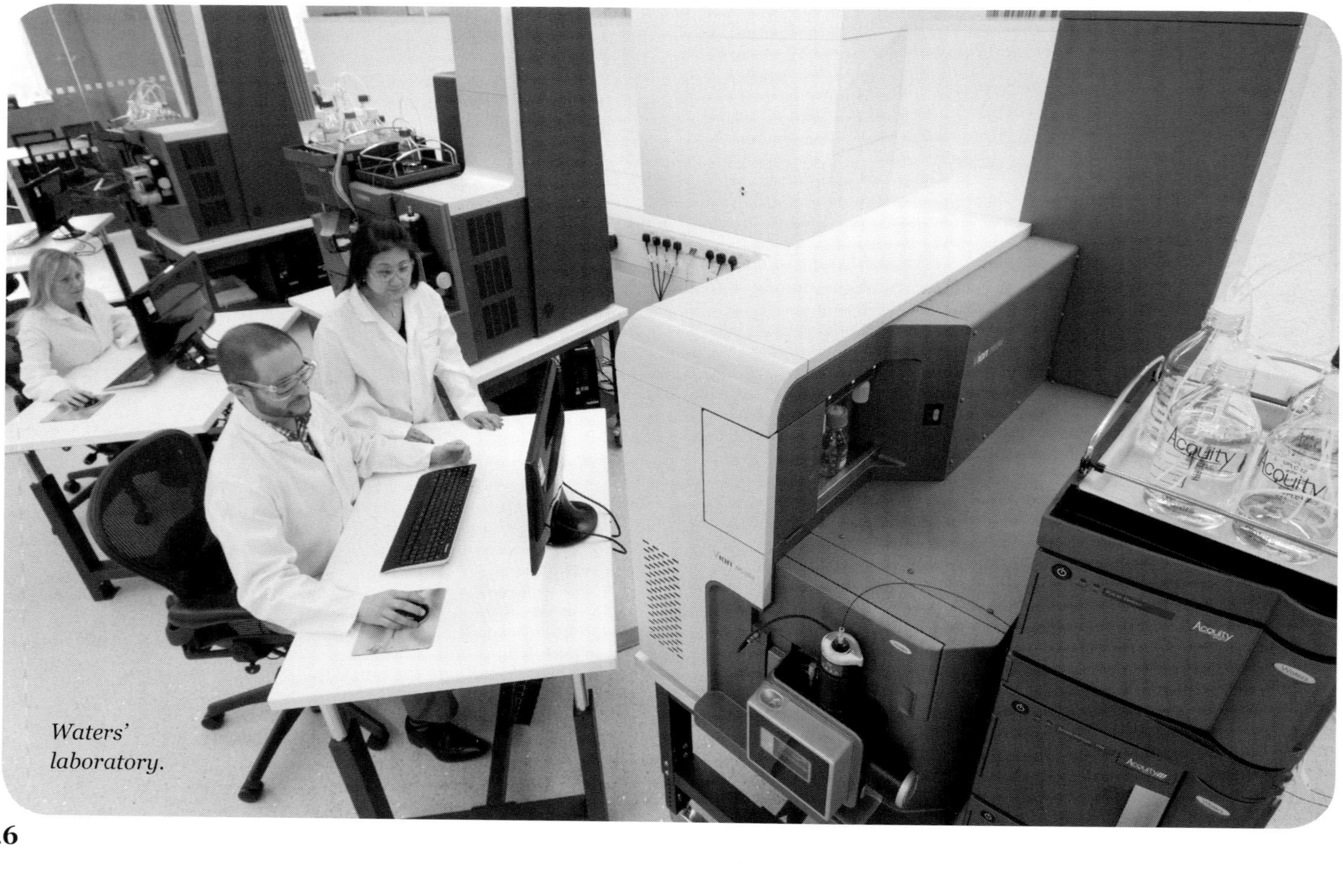

Waters' laboratory.

Left and above: *Waters new state-of-the-art headquarters in Wilmslow.* ***Below:*** *CEO, Chris O'Connell.*

Innovations across several scientific fields - which have a huge impact on our quality of life, safeguarding our food and water supplies - will be supported, including Health Sciences, an area Waters is particularly committed to supporting as we enter a healthcare revolution focused on improving patient care through molecular-level science. This will help with the prevention, diagnosis and treatment of diseases which will be a central pillar of Waters' long-term focus.

Waters has grown to employ 7,000 people globally with 630 based at the Wilmslow site which covers 37 acres. It brought under one roof four operating sites from around Manchester – Floats Road (research and development and manufacturing), Tudor Road (manufacturing and distribution), Atlas Park (demonstration and administration) and Crewe Road (inorganic analysis including ICP, isotope ratio MS and Autospec magnetic sector instruments).

The Wilmslow facility has been designed to drive the next era of innovation through greater collaboration by providing experts a hub from which to create and share new discoveries.

Waters operates in 31 countries and has 15 manufacturing facilities with products available in more than 100 countries, and the Wilmslow site will continue to play an important role in its future.

In the 20+ years since Waters became a public company in 1995, it has earned accolades from customers and investors alike under the leadership of current Chairman, President and Chief Executive Officer Chris O'Connell.

For six decades, Waters Corporation has combined technological leadership with unequalled application and technical support to ensure successes worldwide.

LANXESS
At the heart of the chemical industry

The German-based global speciality chemical company LANXESS is now firmly established at Trafford Park following the 2017 acquisition of U.S. company Chemtura. When the Trafford Park facility opened at Christmas 1939, it was to manufacture phosphate-based plasticizers for Geigy Colour Co Ltd, a subsidiary of Geigy S.A.

The following decades brought changes in ownership and in 1953 it became known as Ashburton Chemicals until another reorganisation occurred and it became an operating site of Geigy (UK) Ltd. In 1970 Geigy SA merged with Ciba AG and the site became part of Ciba Geigy UK. FMC Corporation bought the business in 1992 and then sold it to Great Lakes Chemical Corporation in 1999 until, in 2005, Great Lakes Chemical joined with Crompton to become Chemtura.

LANXESS presence in the UK grew substantially after the company's acquisition of the Clean and Disinfect business of U.S.-based chemicals company Chemours in August 2016. Less than a year later, LANXESS successfully completed the acquisition of U.S. company Chemtura, one of the world's leading suppliers of flame retardant and lubricant additives. Flame retardant and lubricant additives are the main pillars of Chemtura's business and they now complement the current LANXESS portfolio combined in a new Additives business unit.

Above: *Headquarters LANXESS Tower in Cologne.*

The activities of LANXESS in the UK include several production sites, in a broad range of activities. From the blending of inorganic pigments, the manufacturing of science-based biocidal products to the production of urethane prepolymers; plastic additives and flame retardants amongst others.

Throughout the years the research facility at Trafford Park has developed a wide range of new products in fine chemicals and pharmaceutical intermediates, plastic additives and flame retardants, which formed the basis of its operations for several years. For the past 20-plus years, operations have been consolidated into flame retardants, lubrication/hydraulic fluid additives and water-treatment chemicals.

Above: *The old LANXESS site at Trafford Park.* ***Right:*** *A general view of the LANXESS site, June, 1944.*

Above and Right: *LANXESS Trafford Park site.*

The hydraulic/turbo fluids are used in power generation and lubrication applications where flame retardancy is required. The water-treatment additives prevent scale in industrial water and desalination systems.

Research and development plays a significant role at LANXESS, increasing it's competitiveness and expanding business through the development of innovative processes and products as well as the ongoing optimisation of existing production processes. Efforts are directed towards developing new processes, integrating new technologies into existing production processes and conducting efficiency projects to achieve cost and technology leadership.

These main pillars of business have been combined with the LANXESS additives portfolio business unit. This enlarged unit projects LANXESS into a major world player in what is a growing market and the Trafford Park facility is now part of a company which has around 19,200 employees in 25 countries.

Above: *The LANXESS laboratory, 1960's.*

All these activities are closely allied to the needs of the market and the customers. The common goal at LANXESS is the successful execution of research and development projects from the first idea to the finished product. In addition to the development of new products the company also focuses on new applications for existing products as well as on product modifications

Today, LANXESS is looking to the future with clear goals and strategies to ensure profitable growth is sustainable in the years ahead. It says in an increasingly volatile political and economic environment, values-based, responsible and reliable business conduct is more important than ever before. Through its business activities it is committed to taking account of the demands of economics, ecology and society, which reflects its conviction that the company products and expertise can make a significant contribution to supporting its customers, protecting the environment and improving the quality of life for people everywhere.

The Morson Group
Global recruitment specialists

Morson was founded in 1969 by Salford born, Gerry Mason, (right) the father of the current CEO Ged Mason in the family home in Eccles, just a short distance away from the site of the current headquarters. With a background as a mechanical design draughtsman, Gerry Mason spent time in Canada design consignments and managing a branch office for a contract design organisation out of Toronto. It was here he gained valuable experience in business development and management and returned to the UK with his family after three years to start his engineering recruitment business. Right from the outset of the business, Gerry had the burning ambition to be the best in their sector. He firmly believed that passion and ambition coupled with integrity would be the driving force for success.

The first placement was a structural engineer assigned to ICI in Runcorn, Cheshire. In August 1970, the company moved to Bank Chambers on Church Street, Eccles. Soon larger contracts were obtained, not least one at Ashmore, Benson & Pease for 30-plus piping and mechanical designers. Gerry would eventually put the company on the map with upwards of 500 contractors. Apart from the usual challenges of starting a new business, with little funding, and breaking into a sector dominated by several established and fairly large competitors, Gerry soon put his stamp on the sector.

Before long, Morson was beginning to make a mark in the sector providing skilled engineers, designers and draughtsmen on temporary placements across many different industries. With the signing of bigger clients, in order to continue to grow as a business, the company had to move out of the family home and into a permanent office space and take on more employees. Shortly afterwards, Gerry eventually made a bid for larger premises on Clarendon Road, which would be their home for the larger part of two decades.

In 1979 there was a significant development for Morson with the foundation of sister company Morson Projects, their design engineering and project management company, who today have their office based in Irlam.

Morson's first branch office opened in Whitehaven in 1985, and the following year Gerry's son Ged Mason joined the business. Ged, who started in the business as a 'brew boy', to gain experience in all departments, was taking his first steps on his way to the top.

Above: *Stableford Hall, Monton.*

Morson Presented With Ministry of Defence Gold Award

The ERS Gold Awards recognise employers who actively support the Armed Forces community in their workplace and also encourage others to follow their lead. The award scheme, which attracts entries from companies in every part of the country and in the private and public sectors, has seen a rapid increase in participation since it launched in 2014.

In February 2018 it was announced that forces veteran Andy Reid (left) is to become the first Morson Ambassador.

Corporal Andy Reid lost both his legs and right arm after stepping on an IED plate whilst serving with the 3rd Battalion the Yorkshire Regiment in Afghanistan in 2009. After spending only 2 weeks in hospital before returning home after his injury, Andy is a testament to overcoming adversity with a positive mindset.

He was chosen as a Morson Ambassador as his determination, optimism and integrity means that he is a role model, not only for the ex-forces, but for the wider community. At Morson, they are sure he will be an inspiration for candidates, clients and staff.

Left: *Morson Head Office, Adamson House.*

In 1990, Morson once again moved offices to meet growing demand, this time to Stableford Hall in Monton.

The company was awarded it's first 'Managed Vendor' contract with British Energy and in 1995 celebrated a turnover of £50million with 2,000 contractors on the books, some of whom had been with the company since its early days.

Ged Mason took over the helm of the business when his father moved abroad in 1997.

In 2005 he became CEO, with business development director Dr Kevin Gorton taking over as managing director.

In 2006, Morson floated on the stock market for the first time and became Morson Group plc, remaining so until a buyback in 2012.

After once again outgrowing their offices, in 2010 Morson moved to a brand new purpose-built head office building in Adamson House.

Ged Mason, the Group's CEO says: "Manchester has always been a fantastic place to conduct business. From our first office at our family home on New Lane, Salford, to our corporate headquarters on Centenary Way, Salford, we have enjoyed working within the diverse and exciting business culture Manchester provides and we are proud of our roots."

In 2013, the Group acquired Vital Human Resources Ltd and in 2015 reached 12,000 contractors.

In late 2017, Morson further strengthened their presence in IT recruitment, with the acquisition of Leeds-based company The Bridge (IT Recruitment). A further acquisition in January 2018 saw our presence expand in North America with the acquisition of CTSNA.

Named as the UK's No.1 Technical Recruiter, Morson International excels in the provision of effective, impactful recruitment solutions and has helped candidates with their engineering job search since it was established.

Delivering to a broad spectrum of the engineering industry's sectors, Morson has evolved alongside its clients to offer a full recruitment service. Core job sectors include aerospace & defence, rail, power, nuclear, oil & gas, automotive & motorsport, I.T. telecoms and science & pharmaceutical.

Below: *Morson Group staff.*

Ged's massive interest in sport is reflected in his many sponsorships, including: Co owning Sale Sharks RFU, Salford Triathlon, Paul Nicholls Stables along with up and coming sportsmen and women from the world of boxing, golf and horse racing. He successfully co owns race horses with close friend Sir Alex Ferguson, combining his two sporting passions of football and horse racing.

At the heart of their Core Values, charity is of fundamental importance to Morson and its employees and over the last decade we have raised over £1 million for dozens of charitable organisations across the country.

The Morson Charity Committee was founded in 2007, and each year employees vote to select two charitable organisations to raise vital funds for - one local organisation and one national. In 2017, they raised £115,000 for The Christie and Alzheimer's Society.

Morson also has a long history with the Seashell Trust, a North West based charity which provides a happy and secure environment for children and young adults with complex and severe disabilities. Fundraising rea-ched record levels in 2016 as Morson raised £150,000 for Seashell Trust and Springhill Hospice.

Morson Group CEO awarded OBE at Buckingham Palace

Morson Group CEO, Ged Mason, accepted his OBE at Buckingham Palace during a ceremony which took place one day after Her Majesty the Queen's 90th birthday on 22 April, 2016.

He received his OBE from Prince William on a memorable occasion, for services to engineering and design, in a ceremony which celebrates the achievements of remarkable people from across the UK.

With offices now worldwide, Morson celebrates 50 years in business in 2019 and has planned a range of celebratory events throughout the year. Ged Mason said, "I'm very proud of the Morson family and where we are now. As much as we are looking back as we celebrate our birthday, it's important that we look forward and keep driving on, at all times remembering that our greatest asset is our people. As my father used to say, 'there is no finish line, and that is the challenge."

ACKNOWLEDGMENTS

The publishers would like to thank all the individuals and organisations for their help and contribution in respect of this publication.